Welcome to

Kindle
for Beginners

Amazon's Kindle has revolutionised the way in which we read. No longer is it necessary to take up valuable space with shelves full of books, or to keep popping to the shops to pick up the latest newspaper. Now you can receive your daily news digitally, and your entire collection of literature can be stored on a device that you can take everywhere with you. If you're new to the world of Kindle, or you don't think you're familiar with everything that the device has to offer, then **Kindle for Beginners** is the perfect guide to help you learn all there is to know about one of the most popular e-readers in the world. Through easy-to-follow step-by-step tutorials and features, we'll show you how to make the most of this incredible piece of hardware. From connecting to the internet and buying your first eBook to playing games and even browsing the web on your device, everything you need to know about your Kindle is included within these 180 pages. Now let's get started…

Kindle
for Beginners™

Imagine Publishing Ltd
Richmond House
33 Richmond Hill
Bournemouth
Dorset BH2 6EZ
☎ +44 (0) 1202 586200
Website: www.imagine-publishing.co.uk
Twitter: @Books_Imagine
Facebook: www.facebook.com/ImagineBookazines

Editor in Chief
Aaron Asadi

Production Editors
Dan Collins, Amy Squibb

Senior Art Editor
Danielle Dixon

Printed by
William Gibbons, 26 Planetary Road, Willenhall, West Midlands, WV13 3XT

Distributed in the UK & Eire by
Imagine Publishing Ltd, www.imagineshop.co.uk. Tel 01202 586200

Distributed in Australia by
Gordon & Gotch, Equinox Centre, 18 Rodborough Road, Frenchs Forest,
NSW 2086. Tel + 61 2 9972 8800

Distributed in the Rest of the World by
Marketforce, Blue Fin Building, 110 Southwark Street, London, SE1 0SU.

ISBN 978 1908222701

C⊘ntents

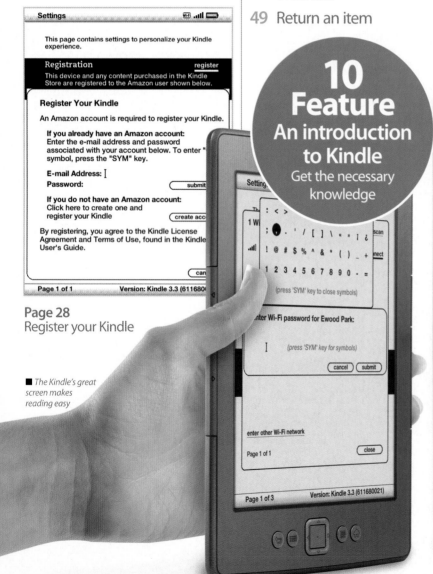

Page 28
Register your Kindle

■ *The Kindle's great screen makes reading easy*

10
Feature
An introduction to Kindle
Get the necessary knowledge

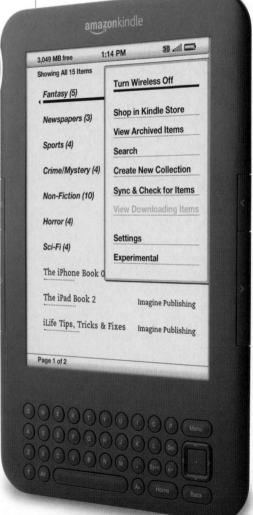

Key pick
Page 124
Use our four-page guide to surf the internet with your Kindle!

Using your Kindle

Page 70
Access and navigate your eBook collection

158
Helpdesk
Kindle solutions
We answer the most frequently asked questions

The next step

Helpdesk

■ *The Kindle Keyboard makes navigation simple*

Getting started

Discover what your Kindle has to offer with our in-depth guides and tutorials

26

■ Connecting to Wi-Fi enables you to buy all the eBooks you could ever need

Page 28

■ Register for an Amazon account to access countless books

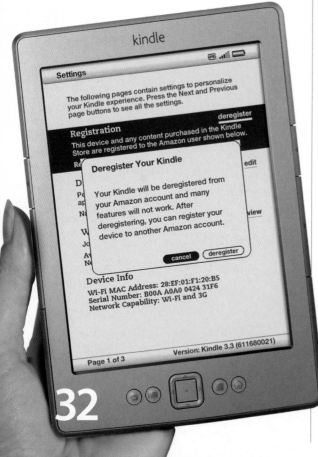

32

Page 34

■ Turn on the 1-Click Payment Method for easy purchasing

"Before long, the advantages of reading on a Kindle come thick and fast"

Key pick
Page 10
Get to know what your Kindle is capable of with our 16-page guide

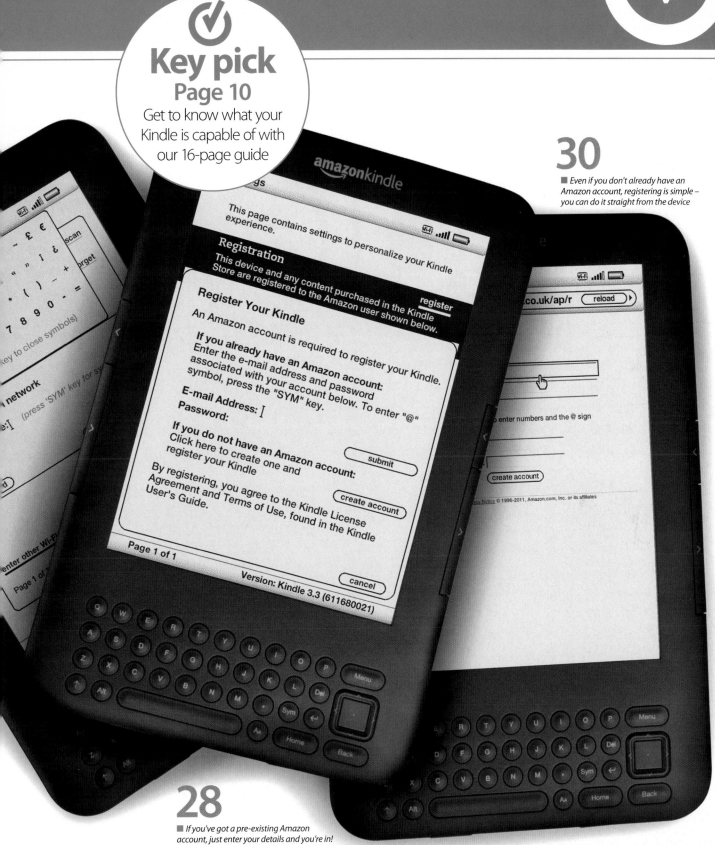

30
■ Even if you don't already have an Amazon account, registering is simple – you can do it straight from the device

28
■ If you've got a pre-existing Amazon account, just enter your details and you're in!

An introduction to
Kindle

Welcome to the wonderful world of reading as you have never experienced it before – through a Kindle! If you have just got your hands on one of these wondrous devices then allow us to guide you through everything you need to know

Slide and release the power sw

If you've been living in outer space for the past few years and have no idea what a Kindle is or what it does, then prepare to be amazed. Kindles are digital e-readers, which means they are devices that you use to read digital books and act as portable, convenient alternatives to the printed, physical books that you know and love. There are many benefits to reading books through a

Kindle, not least the environmentally friendly, tree-saving one. Once connected to a wireless network, you can browse for new books online via the Kindle Store (which is accessible straight from your device) and, provided you have registered your device to an Amazon account, any books you buy will be delivered straight to your device within 60 seconds, without you ever having to leave the house.

Then there is the sleek design of Kindles that make them so intuitive to use and so comfortable to read on. To look at, the words you see on a Kindle screen are indistinguishable from the printed page as the Kindle's high-contrast E-Ink display delivers clear, crisp text and images. You don't have to worry about screen glare from reading in direct sunlight either, meaning that a Kindle is

5 things you need to know

01: Get books in under a minute
With fast, free, wireless delivery, you can start reading eBooks in less than 60 seconds, no computer required.

02: Lighter than a paperback
At only 247g, the Kindle Keyboard is lighter than a paperback and thinner than a magazine. The Kindle 4 even more so.

03: They hold up to 3,500 books
The 4GB storage capacity means that a Kindle Keyboard can store up to 3,500 books and the Kindle 4 up to 1,400.

04: Long battery life
On a single charge and with limited daily use, a Kindle Keyboard will run for up to two months and a Kindle 4 up to a month.

05: Read in bright sunlight
Kindle screens read like real paper with absolutely no screen glare, unlike smartphones and tablets.

the ideal companion to take on holiday and enjoy on the beach or by the pool.

There are two main types of Kindle available: the Kindle Keyboard 3G and the standard Kindle 4. The 3G comes with an integrated physical keyboard, making it quick and easy to enter settings, apply your own notes to readings and search the Kindle Store. As the name suggests, it also comes with 3G as well as Wi-Fi connectivity – and the 3G service is totally free, so you can browse online and get books delivered straight to your device anywhere in the world. The Kindle 4 lacks the keyboard, but its sleeker, lighter design means that it's even more comfortable to read on and its lower price makes it even easier on the wallet. Now read on to find out much more about these fantastic devices.

The ultimate in elegance

We respect that there will always be people who prefer actual physical books over digital ones, with actual flickable pages, the smell of the paper and, in some cases, colour pictures. But when people who haven't tried reading using a Kindle device try to imagine how the process of reading a physical book and a digital book will differ, they picture large, heavy, slab-like machines that do a poor impression of a physical book when you're trying to read them in sunlight – but nothing could be further from the truth. The lightweight design, sleek ergonomics and general all-round comfort ensure that within a few pages you'll have forgotten how you're reading books and just get lost in the actual act of reading itself.

Before long, though, the advantages of reading on a Kindle come thick and fast. How often, for example, have you been lying in bed, with one arm around a loved one and the book in the other? All's well until you need to turn the page, in which case you'll either need dextrous digits like ET to perform the act with one hand or you'll risk inadvertently getting your partner in a headlock while trying

> "Before long, the advantages of reading on a Kindle come thick and fast"

to reach across to use the other hand. But Kindles are designed to be read in one hand, and the button arrangement is such that you can advance or go back pages simply by pressing the paddle buttons on the side of the device. What's more, the soft-touch, textured back makes a Kindle pleasant to hold and you'll never have to worry about the device getting hot in your hands.

Instant access

Utilising Amazon's Whispernet technology, Kindles enable you to wirelessly search, discover and download content on the go. By connecting to a Wi-Fi wireless network, you can browse the extensive selection of »

First steps

So you've just got your Kindle? Here we guide you through the first steps needed to start up and set up your device

Turn your Kindle on

Turning on your Kindle 3 or 4 is as easy as pressing or sliding the power button. Here's how…

01: The power button or switch is located on the underside of your device, so press it or slide it to power up your device.

02: The light next to the switch will illuminate and your device will fire up, ready for action.

Turn your Kindle off

Your Kindle will go into standby mode if left idle for a while, but here's how to turn it off fully…

01: To turn your device off completely, slide and hold the power switch for four to seven seconds until the screen goes blank.

02: You can put your device into sleep mode by sliding the switch, after which a full-screen image will appear on the display.

Put your Kindle to sleep

Your Kindle device will go to sleep automatically after ten minutes of non-use. Or, to do it manually…

01: To put your Kindle into sleep mode, slide the power switch across and then release it.

Slide the Power switch for Sleep mode or to turn off

> "You can put your device to sleep by sliding the switch"

02: A full-screen image will appear and other keys and buttons will become locked so you don't accidentally change the place in your reading.

Charge your Kindle

Although the battery charge of your Kindle is impressive, you will need to charge it up eventually

01: Using the supplied USB cable, plug the smaller end into the micro-USB/power port located on the underside of your device.

02: If you don't have a computer then you can also plug the USB end of the cable into a compatible wall socket to charge the device.

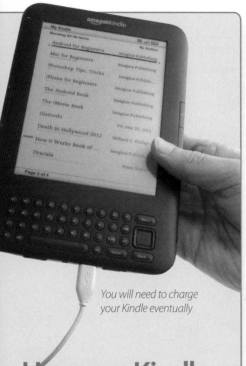
You will need to charge your Kindle eventually

Use your Kindle while charging

You can still use your Kindle while it is charging to a computer and continue to read or shop

01: When your device is plugged into a power source, a message will appear on your device's screen telling you what to do.

02: Simply eject your device from your computer and the screen will 'wake up', allowing you to continue using it as normal.

Set your language

The first time you turn on your Kindle, the Set Up Your Kindle guide will help you set it up

01: Use the five-way controller to navigate the options and select your preferred language from the list provided.

02: Once you have chosen a language, select 'OK' on the pop-up screen to confirm your language preference.

Kindle FAQs

How do I connect to a wireless network?

This is really simple, regardless of which Kindle device you are using. Press the Menu button and then use the five-way controller to navigate down to 'Settings'. Now navigate down to the 'Wi-Fi Settings' section and then your device will scan for activate networks. Select one to join.

My Kindle shows a different name. How do I register/deregister my Kindle?

To register your Kindle, press the Home button, then press Menu. Select 'Settings' and then select 'Register' or 'Deregister'. You can also register or deregister your Kindle via the 'Manage Your Kindle' page on the Amazon website.

Does Kindle come with a backlight?

Kindle's E-Ink display isn't backlit. Unlike traditional backlit displays, E-Ink displays are ideally suited for reading because they do not create the same eyestrain as reading from a computer screen or mobile phone.

Are there any free books?

With thousands of titles, the Kindle Store contains the largest selection of the books people want to read. This includes the most popular classics for free, with wireless delivery in less than 60 seconds to your Kindle, computer or other mobile device.

Can I change the screensaver on my Kindle?

Kindle devices come with pre-installed screensaver images that display when the device is in sleep mode. Unfortunately the devices do not support the use of custom screensavers.

Can I share content with other Kindles?

You can enjoy Kindle content on Kindle devices or applications that are registered to your Amazon account. There may be limits on the number of devices (usually six) that can simultaneously use a single book. Subscriptions to newspapers or periodicals cannot be shared on multiple devices. You can see all your Kindle content and send downloads to your registered Kindle devices or Kindle applications from Your Kindle Library through the 'Manage Your Kindle' section of the Amazon website.

Get your Kindle all set up and start reading

Getting started

>> digital literature on the Kindle Store and then get them downloaded and installed on your device within 60 seconds. And even if you don't have access to Wi-Fi, you can still get books delivered to your device. All Kindle devices can be connected up to a computer with the supplied USB cable and you can buy content from the Kindle Store on the Amazon website and then manually copy it to your connected device. If you have a Kindle 3 (aka Kindle Keyboard), then downloading fresh content is never an issue because the device comes with free 3G coverage, so you can shop and receive delivery of books anywhere in the world without having to worry about eating into data plans and paying out additional costs of any sort.

Portability

Kindles are very, very light – the Kindle Keyboard weighs in at a meagre 247g and the Kindle 4 a paltry 170g, making both considerably lighter than a standard paperback. When you factor in that the 4GB of storage space present in the Kindle Keyboard can hold up to 3,500 books and the 2GB of the Kindle 4 up to 1,400, that's virtually an entire library that you can lug around at any given time. It provides an immense catalogue of digital books at your fingertips whenever you need them – and no trees were harmed in harnessing all those words!

The slim dimensions also mean that both devices can be carried around easily – the Kindle Keyboard can be chucked in your bag and the Kindle 4's 166 x 114 x 8.7mm dimensions mean it is small enough to fit in your pocket, so there really is no excuse not to have it to hand wherever you go. And as for holidays? Well, Kindles love to travel and can be read absolutely everywhere – including by the pool or on the beach in the brightest sunshine imaginable. The high-contrast E-Ink display delivers clear, crisp text and images and the lack of a backlight means that your digital books read like real paper and your reading experience isn't hampered by screen glare caused by reflected sunlight. Charging your device is easy too. A supplied USB cable allows you to connect it to your computer to charge or you can plug the cable into a compatible mains adaptor. But what if you don't have a foreign mains adaptor to use on holiday if you're planning a sunshine trip away? Who cares – you won't need one! Once fully charged, Kindle Keyboards can last up >>

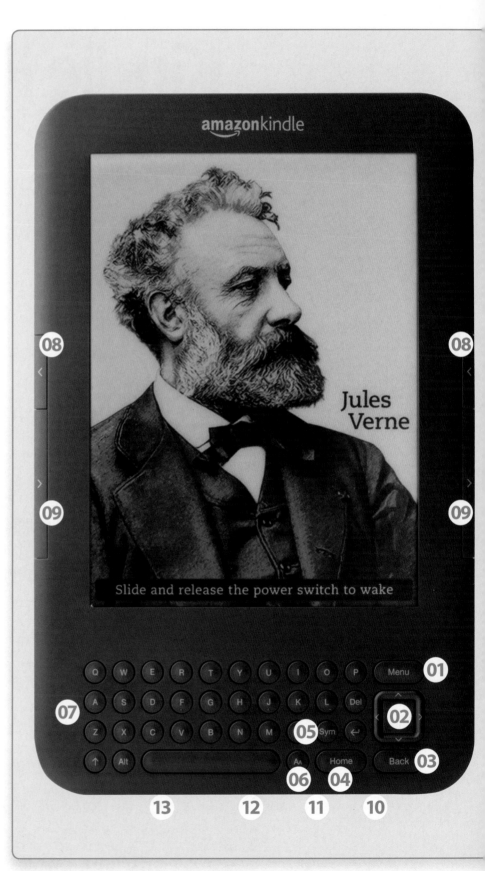

Kindle Keyboard

The Kindle Keyboard device has the advantage of a physical keyboard for faster typing of notes and keywords

If you are serious about reading digital books then the Kindle 3 (aka the Kindle Keyboard and Kindle 3G) is an inviting piece of kit, boasting many features that the Kindle 4 does not. The most obvious is the inclusion of an integrated keyboard, which makes it quick and easy to enter keywords when searching for books and apply your own notes to your digital books.

But that's only the tip of the iceberg because the Kindle 3 also boasts free 3G wireless networking. All Kindle devices can be connected up to a Wi-Fi network to make searching for, buying and receiving books easy, but what if you're out and about and have no access to a Wi-Fi network? Can you still obtain books then? Absolutely! With free 3G wireless networking you can search and buy books any time, any place without having to worry about annual contracts and monthly fees. As such, you can be travelling the world and still get books delivered straight to your device in under 60 seconds!

The device is also much lighter than a standard paperback, has enough storage capacity to hold up to 3,500 books and can hold a battery charge for anything up to two months, making it the ultimate travel companion for people who like to read.

Find your way around

01: **Menu button** This displays the application and navigation choices that are related to the screen you are viewing.

02: **Five-way controller** You use this to navigate between options by pressing a direction to move the on-screen cursor around and selecting an option by pressing the middle button inwards.

03: **Back button** This retraces your steps, like pressing the Back button on a web browser. Press this to go back to the previous screen.

04: **Home button** Press this to view content stored on your Kindle device as well as content archived at Amazon.

05: **Symbol key** This will call up a virtual menu of digits and symbols that aren't present on the standard keyboard. Select them using the five-way controller.

06: **Text key** This changes the size of the text and the words per line while reading and presents available controls for Text-to-Speech.

07: **Keyboard** You can use the keyboard to enter search terms and add notes and URLs for websites, etc.

08: **Previous Page button** You use this to navigate between options by pressing a direction to move the on-screen cursor around and selecting an option by pressing the middle button inwards.

09: **Next Page button** Press either of the two larger flipper buttons to turn the page and advance through your reading material.

10: **Power switch** Slide this button to put your Kindle to sleep, wake it up or turn it on or off.

11: **Micro-USB/Power port** This is where you attach the USB cable that comes bundled with your device to connect it to your computer or a power source to charge your device.

12: **Headphone jack** Plug in your headphones here to listen to an audiobook, background music or content read aloud through Text-to-Speech.

13: **Volume control** Alter the headphone or speaker volume for audiobooks, background music or content read aloud via Text-to-Speech.

5 unique selling points of Kindle Keyboard

01: Tighter dimensions
When it was launched, the Kindle Keyboard was 21 per cent smaller than the Kindle 2 (190 x 213 x 8.5mm) and 15 per cent lighter (at 247g), making it considerably more portable.

02: A more efficient reader
The keyboard action has been tweaked for better tactility and the E-Ink display means that pages turn 20 per cent faster, so the wait for new pages to refresh is minimal.

03: Expand your collections
The internal storage of the Kindle Keyboard has been expanded to 4GB, twice that of its predecessor, allowing enough capacity for up to 3,500 books to be stored within.

04: Free 3G
The Kindle 3 comes with free 3G wireless network access, so you can still shop online at the Kindle Store from anywhere and don't have to worry about annual contracts and monthly fees.

05: Two-month battery life
A single charge for the Kindle 3 can keep its battery running for up to two months, based on the wireless facilities being turned off and half an hour a day of reading time.

The Kindle Keyboard is an impressive device

Getting started

to two months (with wireless connectivity turned off, and based upon half an hour of daily reading time) and Kindle 4s up to a month before requiring a recharge, so they should have plenty of oomph to keep you entertained for the duration of your trip.

Books, books and more books

You will never have to worry about running out of reading material while using your Kindle. The Kindle Store boasts the biggest selection of any eBook store in the world, with more than 900,000 books, including new releases and bestsellers, available at a minute's notice. There's more than books available

as well, with a great selection of digital newspapers and magazines to download, plus blogs and news feeds to provide plenty of material to dip in and out of during the day. The Kindle Store is great value too. Prices are checked on a daily basis to ensure that they are as low as possible and, as such, it is possible to pick up some great bargains while browsing the never-ending virtual bookshelves. Searching the Store is easy, with basic 'Books', 'Newspapers' and 'Magazines' sections serving as gateways to far more extensive search options and categories to help you find what you want in a flash. If you come across a publication of interest then you don't have to commit to a sale straight away: you can opt to download a free sample >>

Type with confidence

Getting to know your Kindle's keyboard

The integrated keyboard of the Kindle 3 makes it quick and easy to enter details when setting up your device as well as add your own notes to your reading material. Included on the keyboard are a few keys with special functions…

In more detail

01: Symbol key If you need numbers, a punctuation mark or a symbol that is

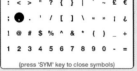

(press 'SYM' key to close symbols)

not shown, press the Symbol key and use the five-way controller to select the desired symbol.

02: Shift key The keyboard enters lower-case letters by default. If you want caps then you can hold the Shift key or press it once to make the next letter capitalised.

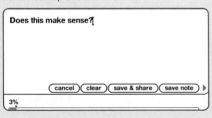

Does this make sense?

cancel   clear   save & share   save note

3%

03: Delete key If you wish to delete text then press the 'Del' key to erase individual letters or hold it down to delete words quickly.

04: Return key To start a new line of text, press the Return key, exactly as you would on a computer keyboard.

05: Text key Changes the size of text and the words per line while reading, alters screen rotation and shows controls for Text-to-Speech.

Aa Aa Aa Aa Aa Aa **Aa Aa**

Typeface	regular	condensed	sans serif
Line Spacing	small	medium	large
Words per Line	fewest	fewer	default
Text-to-Speech	turn on		
Screen Rotation	A A A A		

5 unique selling points to the Kindle 4

01: The lightest Kindle ever
Weighing in at less than 170g, the Kindle 4 is lighter than a paperback and fits snugly into your pocket for easy portability.

02: Read in sunlight
The Kindle 4's E-Ink screen reads like real paper and can be viewed in bright sunlight with no screen glare.

03: Good to go
The Kindle 4 is ready to use right out of the box, with no setup, no software to install and no computer required to get going.

04: Holds up to 1,400 books
The 2GB of internal storage is enough for up to 1,400 books – that's plenty to keep you going over your holiday!

05: One-month battery life
A single charge for the Kindle 4 can keep its battery running for up to a month, based on the wireless facilities being turned off and half an hour a day of reading time.

The Kindle 4 is highly portable yet capacious

Kindle 4

The easy-to-use, keyboardless Kindle 4 is the most compact and portable Kindle device yet

If you're new to digital literature and are in the market for a basic reader that is compact, portable and brimming with features, the Kindle 4 is a sound investment that caters for all basic reading needs. The reservations most people have about reading eBooks is that the process becomes problematic in direct sunlight due to screen glare. However, with the Kindle 4's high-contrast E-Ink display, text and images are clear and crisp and books read just like real paper with no glare whatsoever.

Easy to use right out of the box, the Kindle 4 has enough storage capacity to hold up to 1,400 books and can run up to an entire month on a single battery charge. What's more, the Kindle 4 is the lightest, most compact Kindle ever, ensuring that it is both comfortable to

hold and can be slipped into your pocket easily. The device also comes with free cloud backup, so all of your purchased books are automatically backed up and easily accessible at any time. And although it doesn't boast the

integrated keyboard of the Kindle 3, a simple and intuitive interface means that typing and navigating is never a problem and the lightweight device can be held and used easily with one hand.

Find your way around

01: **Menu button** This displays the application and navigation choices that are related to the screen you are viewing.

02: **Five-way controller** You use this to navigate between options by pressing a direction to move the on-screen cursor around and selecting an option by pressing the middle button inwards.

03: **Back button** This retraces your steps, like pressing the 'back' button on a web browser. Press this to go back to the previous screen.

04: **Home button** Press this to view content stored on your Kindle device, as well as content archived at Amazon.

05: **Keyboard button** This button brings up an on-screen keyboard for entering text. Use the five-way controller to navigate the keyboard and enter search terms, notes and URLs.

06: **Previous Page button** Press either of the two smaller flipper buttons to go to the previous page in your current reading material.

07: **Next Page button** Press either of the two larger flipper buttons to turn the page and advance through your reading material.

08: **Power switch** Press this button to put your Kindle to sleep, wake it up or turn it on or off (press and hold for 7 seconds).

Slide and release the power switch to wake

Getting started

>> instead, which is good for helping you to gauge the style of book and to determine if it is something you would like to read more of.

If it is, then buying books is easy. After connecting your Kindle device to a wireless network (Kindle Keyboards also have free global 3G connectivity, remember) and registering your device to an Amazon account (or creating a new one directly from your device) you're basically good to go, browsing and buying books on your device using Amazon's quick and easy 1-Click Payment service. This means that by storing details of a payment card in your account, you can buy what you want, when you want in a single

> ## "All of your purchases are automatically backed up to the cloud"

click, eradicating the need for navigating through an endless succession of screens in order to get to a virtual checkout, confirming payment and so on – you simply browse, click to buy and your book will be installed and ready to read on your device within a minute – now that's service! And all of your purchases are automatically backed up to the cloud, so you never need to worry about losing your books – you can simply re-download them at any time for free.

Speaking of free, the Kindle Store also boasts a rather large selection of free books. When browsing the store you can set whatever search criteria you want, and by browsing all books under the 'free' bracket, a diverse selection of reads will be presented for you to download at a cost of precisely nothing. So even if you spent your last pennies buying the actual Kindle device itself, you'll still never be short of something to read on it.

Read how you want

Everything about the Kindle is designed for ease of use and happy reading. We have already mentioned the button layout that

allows you to hold your device and turn the pages with one hand; well, if you should so wish, you can get Kindle Keyboards to read to you. With built-in Text-to-Speech, you can lean back, close your eyes and give your peepers a rest while audio narrative is read aloud. But your reading options can be tweaked on whatever Kindle device you are using to adjust the size of the font and style to pick something that works for you; the orientation of the page can also be adjusted to how you are holding your device. You view books in a portrait orientation as standard, but if you want to tilt your device on its side and get more words on a line, then that's not a problem – your reading, your rules.

The books you read on Kindles are identical to their physical, printed counterparts, right down to the page numbers, which correspond to print editions so you can easily reference and cite passages. The Kindle Keyboard also boasts a built-in dictionary with instant lookup, so if you stumble across a word that you don't know the meaning of while reading, you can type it into the dictionary and get instant definitions for over 250,000 >>

No keyboard? No problem

Who needs an integrated keyboard when a virtual one is just a button press away?

If you need to enter text when setting up your device or for adding notes or URLs, the lack of a physical keyboard on the Kindle 4 isn't an issue: just press the Keyboard button to call up a virtual keyboard. There are numerous character sets to select and you can navigate around it using the five-way controller.

In more detail

01: Keyboard button Press the Keyboard button to call up the virtual keyboard, then use the five-way controller to select the various characters shown on screen.

02: Keyboard sets There are various keyboard sets available that you can scroll through and select, including lower-case, upper-case and symbols.

Navigating your Kindle
Home screen
Take a guided tour of your Kindle's main entry screen

Like smartphones and tablets, all Kindle devices feature a Home screen – a launch pad from where you can access all of your content and collections stored on the device, including books, newspapers, magazines, blogs, active content and personal documents. The Home screen is the first screen that you will see whenever you turn your device on and you can navigate your way around it using the five-way controller.

Here we will guide you around the various features and menus that appear on your device's Home screen, to help you get to grips with your Kindle device and use it more effectively.

Find your way around

01: **Device name** You can personalise your Kindle by naming it. You can edit this name by pressing the Menu button, choosing 'Settings' and then editing the 'Device Name'.

02: **Sort Options** By selecting this option and pressing left or right on the five-way controller, you can choose which types of content you want displayed on your Home screen.

03: **Titles** The titles of the items listed on your Home screen will be instantly visible. The words 'Sample' and 'New' will be added to samples and content uploaded in the last 24 hours.

04: **Author or date** For books, the author of the item is listed, and for periodicals and blogs, the date is listed next to the corresponding item.

05: **Collections** You can create categories on your Kindle and organise your content accordingly to make it easier to navigate and view your reading material.

06: **Wireless indicator** If you are connected to a Wi-Fi or 3G network then an icon will be visible on the top bar that indicates your network status.

07: **Pages in Home** This indicates the total number of pages in Home. Use the Next Page or Previous Page buttons to navigate to the various pages available.

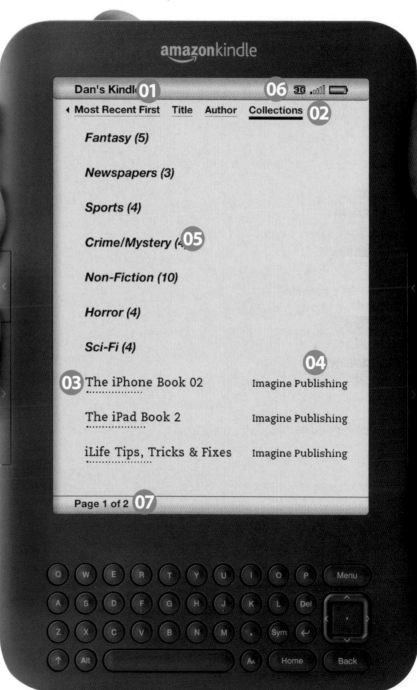

Getting started

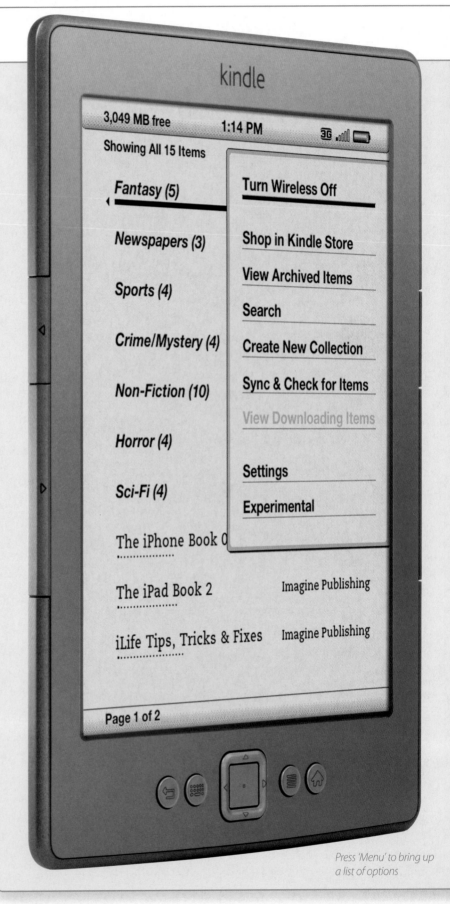

>> English words without interrupting your reading. With built-in Twitter and Facebook integration, Kindle Keyboards also let you share passages with friends and family.

Another good reason to own a Kindle is as a digital file to ferry around all of your important documents. The Kindle Keyboard makes it easy to take your personal documents with you, eliminating the need to print. You and your approved contacts can email documents – including Word, PDFs and more – directly to your Kindle and read them in Kindle format. Your personal documents will be stored in your Kindle library on Amazon and be ready to download conveniently anywhere at any time. You can add notes, highlights and bookmarks, which are automatically synchronised across devices along with the last page you read using Amazon's Whispersync technology. You can read your PDFs in their native format, view them in landscape mode, or zoom in up to 300 per cent to view small print and detailed tables and graphics. You can also convert your PDF documents to the Kindle format so that they reflow like a regular Kindle book.

> ## "Kindle Keyboard makes it easy to take your personal documents with you"

Get experimental

The refreshing thing about Amazon, in regards to its Kindle, is that it's very open about the features currently in development and even lets you try them out to see how well they work and if you think Amazon should continue to develop them at all. These features are accessible in the 'Experimental' section after pressing the Menu button and include all kinds of exciting stuff…

With the Text-to-Speech feature, Kindle Keyboards can read English newspapers, magazines, blogs and books out loud to you, unless the book's rights holder made the feature unavailable. You can switch back and forth between reading and listening, and your spot is automatically saved. Pages automatically turn while the content is being read, so you can listen hands-free. You can choose from both male and female voices, >>

Press 'Menu' to bring up a list of options

Using the Home screen menu

More options are available by pressing the 'Menu' button. Here's a guide to them…

Turn Wireless Off

This option is used to disconnect your Kindle device from a wireless network. Select it using the five-way controller and click the option.

View Archived Items

Selecting this will let you view downloadable items stored at the Amazon website that are not currently on your device.

Settings

You can manage and tweak certain aspects of your device, such as naming it or connecting to Wi-Fi, by selecting the 'Settings' option.

Search

This option allows you to search for items on your Kindle device or in the Kindle Store. You can also search via Google, Wikipedia or on the web.

Create New Collection

To help organise your content you can create a name for a collection, then move items into that collection to make them easier to find.

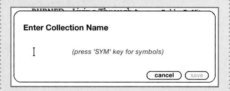

Shop in Kindle Store

Selecting this option will take you to the Kindle Store, provided you are connected to a wireless network, and allow you to start shopping for reading material.

Sync & Check for Items

If you have purchased items from the Amazon website that haven't yet been transferred to your device then you can click this option to sync content immediately.

Experimental

This category is reserved for prototype items that Amazon is currently working on, such as web browsers and MP3 playback, allowing you to try them out.

Getting started

» which can be sped up or slowed down to suit your preference. What if you're in the middle of a great story or article but have to jump in the car? Simply turn on Text-to-Speech and listen on the go. New text-to-speech-enabled menus allow users to navigate their Kindle Keyboard without having to read menu options. In addition to listening to books aloud, users now have the option of listening to content listings on the Home screen, item descriptions and all menu options.

Kindle Keyboards feature an experimental web browser, based on WebKit, to provide a better web browsing experience. Now it's easier than ever to find the information you're looking for right from your Kindle Keyboard. Experimental web browsing is free to use over 3G or Wi-Fi. You can also transfer MP3 files to Kindle Keyboard to play as background music while you read. You can quickly and easily transfer MP3 files via USB by connecting the Kindle Keyboard to your computer and provide your own ambience to your readings.

Your Kindle, your rules

As we have discovered, Kindles are versatile devices that offer a wide array of features and are flexible enough to bend to your own reading rules and whims. We too have had reservations in the past about making the transition from the printed page to the digital format, but within minutes of picking up a Kindle for the first time and seeing just how good a job it does of replicating book pages and spoiling you with additional features, we were converted, and you will be too.

Our advice is to get your hands on your Kindle as soon as possible – round at a friend's house, in a store, anywhere – and try it out for yourself. Once you see how authentic the pages look on screen, experience how easy books are to read through the device – both in terms of comfort and clarity – and then delve into the Kindle Store for the first time to see the wealth of digital literature that is available to own, within seconds, then you'll never go back to paperbacks again. And trees the world over can breathe a sigh of relief!

Using the Kindle's Menu when reading

Pressing the Menu button while reading brings up a new set of options. Here we guide you through them

Go to…

This option allows you to jump to any point in the book. You can enter a page number or select one of the other options such as 'Beginning', 'Cover' and 'End'.

Sync to Furthest Page Read

If you are reading a book across multiple devices, such as your Kindle device and the Kindle iPad or computer apps, triggering this option will mean that you're up to date with the latest point to which you have read across all devices.

Book Description

Selecting this option will connect you to the Kindle Store to get a description of the book you are currently reading.

Search This Book

Selecting this option brings up a search window whereby you can enter keywords and phrases to find the corresponding content in the book.

Add a Bookmark

If you wish to mark a particular point in the book that you are currently reading, this option allows you to do that instantly.

Add a Note or Highlight

You can add your own notes to book text or highlight certain paragraphs by selecting this option and then following the on-screen prompts.

View Notes & Marks

This option allows you view the various notes and highlights that you have applied to a particular book.

"You can add your own notes to book text"

The Menu button leads to many options

Kindle Store FAQs

How do I access the Kindle Store?

You can access it from the Kindle by pressing the Menu button and then using the five-way controller to select the 'Shop in Kindle Store' option. Or go to the Amazon website on your computer and, under the 'Shop All Departments' section at the top left, choose 'Kindle Store' under the 'Kindle' section.

How do I browse the Store on my Kindle device?

At the top of the Kindle Store page are four categories listed under the 'Browse' header. Click on one to start browsing that section – or enter specific keywords, such as the title of a book or an author, into the 'Search' field.

What does the 'Recommended for You' category mean?

These are books that may be of interest to you based on your previous purchases and searches. It's a good way to discover new books that may suit you.

How do I register my Kindle to an Amazon account?

While on your Kindle's Home screen, press the Menu button, then use the five-way controller to scroll down to 'Settings'. Under the 'Registration' heading, click on 'Register', then enter the email address and password for your Amazon account.

How do I purchase books from the Kindle Store on the Amazon website?

If you have registered your device to an Amazon account, log in using that account on the website and then search for books. Once you have found one you like, use the 'Deliver to' drop-down menu at the top right

You can buy eBooks and manage your Kindle account on the Amazon website

to choose your device, then click the 'Buy now with 1-Click' button. Your purchase will be transferred wirelessly to your Kindle, if it's connected to a Wi-Fi network.

Can I buy and transfer books to my Kindle without Wi-Fi?

Yes. Go to the Kindle Store section of the Amazon website and connect your device to your computer using the USB cable. Now, when buying an item, select the 'Transfer via Computer' in the 'Deliver to' drop-down menu and download the item. Now open your Kindle on your desktop, then copy the downloaded file to the 'Documents' folder.

Can I return books and cancel purchases?

Yes. If buying from your device, a 'Purchased by Accident?' option will appear on the

confirmation screen. Click it. To return books from the website, click 'Manage Your Kindle' for a list of bought content, then click 'Actions' and choose 'Return or Refund'.

How do I change my payment settings?

You can set up or edit your '1-Click' payment through the Amazon website by clicking 'Manage Your Kindle'. Then, under the 'Your Kindle Account' section, choose 'Payment Settings'. Your default 1-Click Payment Method will then be displayed in the main window, so click on the 'Edit' link next to it.

Kindle Keyboard shortcuts

If you want to navigate your way around your device quicker then these handy shortcuts are sure to save you time

General shortcuts

There are loads of shortcut 'hotkeys' available to Kindle users that aren't mentioned in the user manual. Some of these shortcuts let you perform certain functions, navigate around your device quicker and even take screenshots of what is displayed on your device (which can then be accessed by connecting it to a computer and opening up the 'Documents' folder). Here we show you the various shortcuts available for general Kindle use.

Alt + Shift + G
Take a screenshot of what is currently displayed on your device.

Alt + G
This will refresh what is currently displayed on your Kindle screen.

Alt + Shift + M
This will allow you to play a hidden Minesweeper game.

Alt + Home
This will take you straight to the Kindle Store.

Alt + top row of keyboard letters
This will allow you to type the numbers 1-9.

Menu
This displays a clock showing the current time on the top bar. It will also display the current available memory in the top-left corner.

Hold the power slide for 15 seconds
This will restart your device – which you can also do by going to Menu>Settings> Menu>Restart.

Reading shortcuts

If you're one of those people who likes to skim-read books and get through them as quickly as possible, there are some hidden shortcuts to help you out. The following selecting of hotkeys only take effect when pressing the corresponding commands

on your Kindle 3's keyboard while reading, but they will certainly save you some time continuously pressing the Next Page button to flick through the various pages and chapters. There are also hidden shortcuts included to activate and disable the Text-to-Speech functions and access your music.

Alt + B
This allows you to instantly add or remove bookmarks without navigating the menu.

Right arrow
Pressing the right arrow on the five-way controller lets you skip to the next chapter.

Left arrow
Pressing the left arrow on the five-way controller lets you skip to the previous chapter.

Shift + Sym
This quick combination allows you to turn Text-to-Speech on or off.

Back
Hitting the Back button will turn off the Text-to-Speech function.

Spacebar
Hitting the spacebar will pause Text-to-Speech when it's active.

Alt + spacebar
Pressing this key combination will turn music on or off.

Alt + F
Pressing this combination will skip to the next music track.

Image viewer shortcuts

Your Kindle device has hidden image viewing capabilities which, although not great, are fun to play around with. To set up the image viewing capabilities, connect your Kindle device to your computer using the USB cable, then open your Kindle from your desktop.

Create a new folder (not inside the other folders) and call it 'Pictures'. Open this folder and create another folder that you can call what you want. Copy images into this folder and disconnect your device, then press Alt + Z on the Home screen to add the newly created image folder to your content list. Click on the new folder and the image view will launch.

Q
Pressing this key enables you to zoom in on an image.

W
Pressing this key enables you to zoom out of an image.

E
Pressing this key enables you to reset the zoom to default.

C
Pressing this key allows you view an image in its actual size.

F
Pressing this key allows you view an image full screen.

R
Pressing this key enables you to rotate an image.

Five-way controller
Pressing directions on the five-way controller allows you to pan an image.

Page Forward/Page Back
Press the Page Forward or Page Back buttons to cycle through images.

Kindle 4 shortcuts

There is no doubt that owning a Kindle Keyboard is by far the quickest and most effective way to navigate around your reading material as the physical keyboard offers numerous shortcuts around the command list which we've already outlined. That's not to say owners of the standard Kindle 4 device have to carry out every action the long convoluted way – there are a handful of hotkey shortcuts available to save you some time navigating the various virtual keyboard commands. Here we present the full list of useful, time-saving button presses. For the keyboard-specific shortcuts, you must first press the Keyboard button to call up your virtual keyboard.

Letter + middle button on five-way controller
Holding the five-way controller button allows you to type a capital letter.

Next Page/Previous Page buttons
Press the large flipper buttons on the side of your device to switch keyboard sets.

Left or Right arrows on five-way controller
Left or right on the five-way controller lets you move seven letters forwards or backwards.

Keyboard Button + Previous Page Button
Pressing this button combination lets you delete a character.

Keyboard Button + Next Page Button
Pressing this button combination lets you insert a space.

Keyboard Button + Back Button
Press these two buttons to refresh the page.

Keyboard Button + Menu Button
Press these buttons and five seconds later you will capture a screenshot.

Left or Right arrows on five-way controller
While reading, pressing left or right on the five-way controller will advance or go back a chapter.

Menu
This displays a clock showing the current time on the top bar. This will also display the current available memory in the top-left corner.

Accessories

Why not splash out on an accessory or two to protect your Kindle, charge it up or make reading on it even more pleasurable?

01: Cases The range of cases is extensive and most provide sleek, lightweight designs that protect your device without adding too much additional bulk. Think of these as sturdy sleeves to keep your Kindle safe that fold back, like a book cover, to provide easy access.

02: Power adaptors Your Kindle comes with a USB cable for connecting to a computer and charging. This cable also works with all standard Apple iPhone and iPad power adaptors, but if you don't have access to one of those and wish to connect your Kindle direct to a plug socket then Amazon Kindle UK produces its own Power Adaptor that is very reasonably priced.

03: Reading lights Kindles don't use backlights, so if you want to read on your Kindle in dimly lit areas you'll need a little extra illumination. There are lots of different lights available that clip onto the top of your device so you can continue reading long into the night without disturbing anybody snoozing.

04: Skins Invest in a skin to snugly encapsulate your Kindle and provide durable scratch protection while allowing you to personalise your device and make it stand out.

05: Sleeves While Kindle cases fold open like books to provide easy access, some of you may prefer the naked feel of the device in your hands, in which case a good option is a protective sleeve that you can easily slip your device in and out of.

06: Replacement cables Although your device comes with a free USB cable to connect your Kindle device up to a computer or power source, you may need a replacement if yours gets lost or damaged. You can buy replacement USB cables that are universal to all Kindle devices directly from Amazon.

07: Mains chargers Rather than buying power adaptors to use with your device's USB cable to plug your Kindle directly to a power source, a cheaper option is to purchase a mains charger. These cost less than a fiver, come with lifetime warranties and work with all possible Kindle devices – ideal for taking on holiday.

Connect to Wi-Fi

Hook your device up to a wireless network and enjoy the benefits of exploring the Kindle Store for great new reads

To get the most out of your Kindle device, you need to connect it to a Wi-Fi network. How else are you going to start browsing the Kindle Store and downloading a wealth of fabulous digital eBooks to get engrossed in?

Your Kindle can wirelessly connect to private Wi-Fi networks in your home or office through your Wi-Fi router, as well as public Wi-Fi hotspots at airports, schools and your favourite cafe, which often offer free access to their networks. Your Kindle automatically detects nearby Wi-Fi networks that broadcast their network name and, thankfully, the process of connecting is very quick and easy, no matter which device you are using.

If your device is brand new, then the initial set-up wizard will guide you through

the procedure of setting up Wi-Fi, but if you wish to connect to a new network later then you simply have to press the Menu button (both on standard Kindle and Kindle Keyboard devices), use the five-way controller to select Settings and then choose Wi-Fi Settings.

The device will scan and detect available networks, so you simply have to highlight the one you wish to connect to and enter any required passwords. You only have to log on once. Once a Wi-Fi network has been connected to, your device will remember it and next time you'll be able to jump straight on with no delays.

In this tutorial we guide you through the initial process of connecting your device to a Wi-Fi network so that you can start getting the most out of your Kindle.

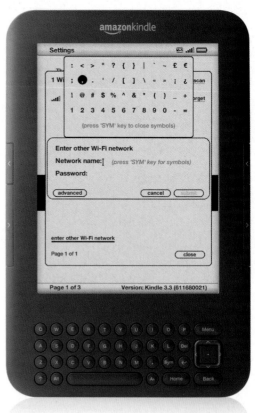

"Your Kindle automatically detects nearby Wi-Fi networks"

Scanning and connecting to Wi-Fi
Get to know your Wi-Fi settings

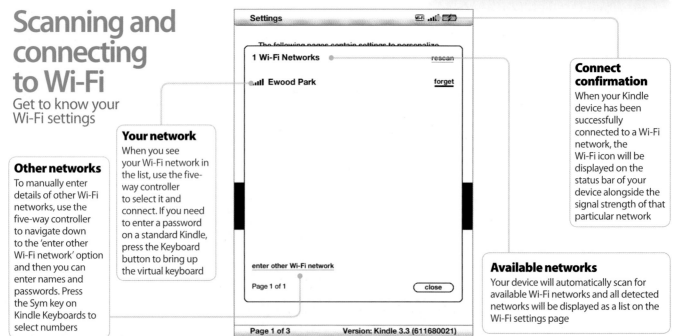

Other networks
To manually enter details of other Wi-Fi networks, use the five-way controller to navigate down to the 'enter other Wi-Fi network' option and then you can enter names and passwords. Press the Sym key on Kindle Keyboards to select numbers

Your network
When you see your Wi-Fi network in the list, use the five-way controller to select it and connect. If you need to enter a password on a standard Kindle, press the Keyboard button to bring up the virtual keyboard

Connect confirmation
When your Kindle device has been successfully connected to a Wi-Fi network, the Wi-Fi icon will be displayed on the status bar of your device alongside the signal strength of that particular network

Available networks
Your device will automatically scan for available Wi-Fi networks and all detected networks will be displayed as a list on the Wi-Fi settings page

01: Go to Settings

You can connect to Wi-Fi as part of the initial set-up process or later if you prefer. To connect to a Wi-Fi network at your convenience, press the Menu key and then navigate to the Settings option. You should now see a section dedicated to Wi-Fi Settings; select this option.

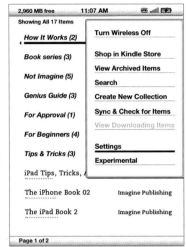

02: Scan for network

You will now be taken to a screen displaying all available Wi-Fi networks. Your device will automatically scan for new networks as soon as this screen is accessed, so ensure that yours is displayed. If not, refer to your Wi-Fi network settings or reset your network before trying again.

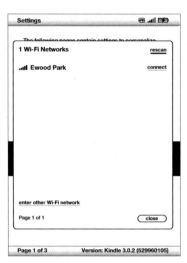

03: Connect to Wi-Fi

When your device has successfully scanned and found your local Wi-Fi network, select it and then click 'connect', enter your password and within a few seconds the set-up process will be complete and you'll be able to start accessing the Kindle online bookstore.

04: WPS Connect

If your Wi-Fi network and router supports WPS technology, your Kindle device will detect it. Press the WPS association button on your router and, on the Kindle, go to Navigate to Connect via WPS and choose the option.

05: Enter your password

If your network does not support WPS technology, enter the Wi-Fi network password by pressing the Keyboard key and selecting the various characters with the five-way controller. If you need to enter digits on your Kindle keyboard then press the Sym button and select the numbers from the floating menu.

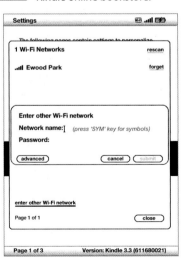

06: Start shopping

Now that your Kindle device is connected to a Wi-Fi network, the Wi-Fi icon will be presented on the status bar and you will be able to connect to the online Kindle store. To start shopping, press the Menu button and then use the five-way controller to select the Shop in Kindle Store option whereby you will be taken to the store front.

Register your Kindle

Make shopping for exciting new reads infinitely easier by registering your Kindle device to your Amazon account

Once you have connected your Kindle device to a Wi-Fi network, the next important step in setting up involves registering your Kindle. Registering your Kindle to an Amazon account enables you to purchase books and other goods as well as use other features – and the process is just as easy through your device as connecting to a network.

When first setting up your Kindle you will be guided through the process by the set-up wizard, but you can register later if you wish. On the device's Settings screen is a section dedicated to Registration. Use the five-way controller to navigate down to this section and highlight and click Register. You will then be taken to a screen where you can either

register your Kindle to an existing Amazon account, or create a new account. When entering the email address and password associated with an existing Amazon account, keep pressing down on the five-way controller to position the cursor next to each entry field and either press the Keyboard button on a standard Kindle to bring up the virtual keyboard, or simply enter the details using a Kindle Keyboard.

Creating a new account is just as easy. You will be taken online to the Amazon Store whereby you'll just need to enter the required details before setting up the account to which your device will be tethered. Once registered, you can start shopping for essential reads.

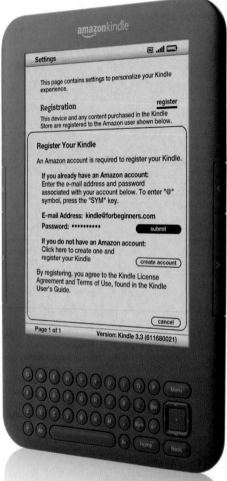

"Registering your Kindle to an Amazon account enables you to purchase books and other goods"

01: Go to Settings

You can register your Kindle as part of the initial set-up process or later if you prefer. To register at your convenience, press the Menu key and then navigate to the Settings option. You should now see a section called Registration.

02: Click to register

Using the five-way controller, navigate to the 'register' option and you will be presented with two main options – to log in to an existing Amazon account or create a new one from your device.

Registering your Kindle

It is easy to tether your Kindle device to your Amazon account

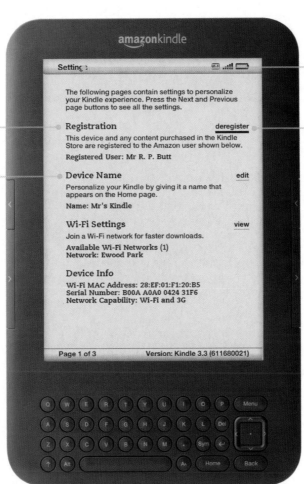

Your settings
The Settings screen consists of three pages of details that relate to your device. The first page is dedicated to your Amazon account and Wi-Fi settings – the most important settings

Registration
Use the five-way controller to navigate down to the 'register' option and then you can log in with your existing Amazon account details or create a new account

Deregistering
If the Kindle you are using is presently registered to someone else's account, then navigate to the 'deregister' option under the Registration section

Device name
To personalise your Kindle device further, you can give it a name. Simply navigate down to the 'edit' option under Device Name and call it what you want

REGISTER ONLINE
You can also register your Kindle on your computer. Simply log in to your Amazon account and then, under your account settings, click on the Register a Kindle option and enter the 16-digit serial number – which you can get from your Kindle's Settings screen under Device Info.

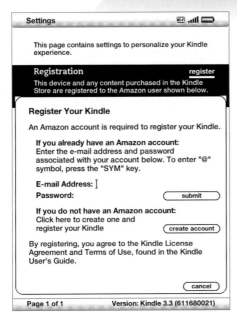

03: Enter details
If you have an existing account, enter the registered email address and password on your Kindle Keyboard. If you are using a standard Kindle device then use the five-way controller to navigate down to each item and then press the Keyboard button.

04: Create account
If you don't have an existing Amazon account then creating one straight from your device is easy. Just select the 'create account' option and then, as long as you are connected to Wi-Fi, enter your details.

Register your Kindle if you don't have an Amazon account

Don't have an existing account? Don't worry, shopping for books through your device is still just minutes away!

Once you've connected your Kindle device to a wireless network, the final steps you need to take just prior to shopping on the online Kindle Store is to register your device to an Amazon account. We've already explored how to register your device to an existing account, but what if you don't have one?

Well, you can create a new account straight from your device. All you have to do is press the Menu button, then use the five-way controller to scroll to 'Settings'. Here you can select the 'Registration' option, which will take you to a screen where you can log into an existing account

or create a new one. Scroll down to 'Create Account' and your device will then connect to the Amazon online store. Choose your country of residence, then enter an active email address, name and password to set up your account. Once done, press the Menu button and then choose the 'Shop in Kindle Store' option to be taken online to the Amazon store. You will be presented with a list of categories, including Books, Newspapers and Magazines as well as handy pointers such as Kindle Best Sellers and New & Noteworthy. So browse at your leisure and discover the wonderful world of reading through your Kindle.

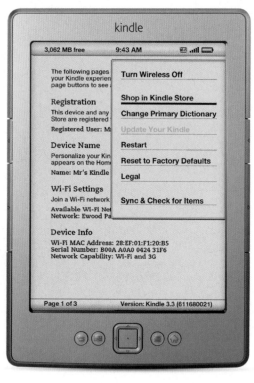

"You can create a new Amazon account straight from your device"

01: Go to Settings

You can register your Kindle as part of the initial setup process or later if you prefer. To register at your convenience, press the Menu key and then navigate to the 'Settings' option. You should now see a section called 'Register'.

02: Click on Register

Using the five-way controller, navigate to the 'Register' option and then you will be presented with two main options – to log into an existing Amazon account or create a new one from your device. Click on 'Create Account'.

Setting up a new account

Creating a new account from your Kindle is easy

Passwords
You will need to protect your account with a password. Create something unique and use letters and digits (press the Sym key to type numbers). You will have to enter the same password twice

Create account
When all of the required fields have been filled, use the five-way controller to scroll down to the 'Create Account' option and then click it to create your new Amazon account and start shopping

START SHOPPING
Now your Kindle is connected to a wireless network and you have registered your device to an Amazon account, you can start shopping online by pressing Menu and then selecting 'Shop in Kindle Store'.

Amazon.co.uk Registration   Wi-Fi

`https://www.amazon.co.uk/ap/r`   reload

amazon.co.uk

Create an Amazon Account

My name is:

My e-mail address is:

Type e-mail again:

Tip: Use the SYM key to enter numbers and the @ sign

Enter a password:

Type password again:

create account

Conditions of Use Privacy Notice © 1996-2011, Amazon.com, Inc. or its affiliates

---

Your name
Enter the name you want associated with your new account here. If using a standard Kindle, press the Keyboard button to bring up a virtual keyboard with which to enter the text

Your email address
Enter an email address that you want to tether to your Amazon account. You will be notified at this address when your account has been set up, as well as receive special offers and alerts

---

03: Create account
Use the five-way controller to navigate down to the 'Create Account' option and you'll be taken online to begin setting up an account. Start the process by clicking on the 'Choose' drop-down menu and then pick your country.

04: Enter personal details
You will now be required to enter your name, email address and a password for your new account. Use the five-way controller to scroll down to each field and then press the Keyboard button (on a standard Kindle) to enter text.

Deregister your Kindle

If you have a second-hand Kindle, you'll want to deregister the existing Amazon account that it's set to

Everybody wants to get their hands on a Kindle. Whether your buy one from new, purchase one second hand or are fortunate enough to be given or loaned one by a friend or family member then you can still make it your own within a matter of minutes. There are a couple of ways to do this – give your device a name that will appear on the Home page, and register it to your own Amazon account so that you can start shopping online at the Amazon Store and downloading piles of lovely e-literature to start reading through your device.

However, what if the Kindle you currently possess is already registered to an Amazon account? Will this prevent you from making your own purchases and getting the most out of your Kindle experience? Not one

bit, because you can easily deregister your device from the account that it is currently tethered to and then enter the details of your own account or even create a brand new account from the device itself.

You can tell whether the Kindle you are using is registered to an existing account by pressing the Menu button and then choosing the 'Settings' option. Under the 'Registration' section, if the device is already registered to an Amazon account then the name of the account holder will be displayed, as will the option to 'Deregister'. By selecting this option you will disconnect the device from the current account and free it up to enter the details of another account. In this tutorial we will guide you through the simple process of deregistering your Kindle.

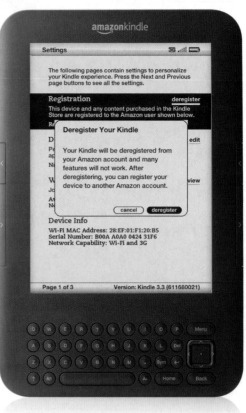

"You can easily deregister your device from the account it is set to"

01: Go to Settings

All aspects of your Kindle's ability to connect with the Amazon Store via Wi-Fi are managed from the main Settings screen, which you can access at any time by pressing the Menu button and then navigating down to the 'Settings' section.

02: Deregister the Kindle

On the Settings screen you will see a section called 'Registration'. If your Kindle device is already tethered to an Amazon account then the name of the account it is registered to will be displayed next to 'Registered User' and the 'Deregister' option will be visible.

Deregistering an account

Untethering your Kindle from an account is easy

Settings Wi-Fi .atl 🔋

The following pages contain settings to personalize your Kindle experience. Press the Next and Previous page buttons to see all the settings.

Registration   *deregister*

This device and any content purchased in the Kindle Store are registered to the Amazon user shown below.

Registered User: Mr R. P. Butt

Device Name   *edit*

Personalize your Kindle by giving it a name that appears on the Home page.

Name: Mr's Kindle

Wi-Fi Settings   *view*

Join a Wi-Fi network for faster downloads.

Available Wi-Fi Networks (1)
Network: Ewood Park

Device Info

Wi-Fi MAC Address: 28:EF:01:F1:20:B5
Serial Number: B00A A0A0 0424 31F6
Network Capability: Wi-Fi and 3G

Page 1 of 3   **Version: Kindle 3.3 (611680021)**

Your settings
All of the options to connect your Kindle to a Wi-Fi network and register it to an Amazon account are accessed by pressing the Menu button and choosing 'Settings'

Deregistering
To disconnect the Kindle from the Amazon account that it is registered to, use the five-way controller to navigate down to the 'Deregister' option and then select it

USING YOUR VIRTUAL KEYBOARD
If using a standard Kindle device, press the Keyboard button to start entering your details. Five keyboard menus are found at the top, including a symbol one at the far left. To close the keyboard, hit 'Done' or press the Keyboard button.

Registered user
The name of the user whose Amazon account is currently tethered to the device will be displayed under the 'Registration' section on your Settings screen

Device name
Don't forget that you can personalise your Kindle still further by giving your device a name that will appear on the Home page – you can do that here

03: Finish the process
Highlight the 'Deregister' option then click the five-way controller button to select it. A message will warn you of the implications of deregistering. If you're still happy to go ahead, select 'Deregister' to finish the process.

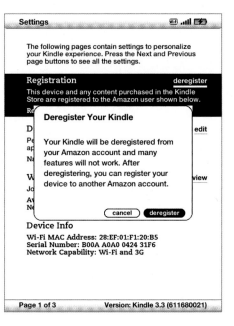

04: Enter new details
You'll be returned to the previous screen where the 'Registered User' field will be clear and the 'Deregister' option will now say 'Register'. Select this, then enter the details of an existing Amazon account or create a new one straight from the Kindle.

Set up your 1-Click Payment Method

Purchasing books through your device is easy and can be set up to take place with a single click. Here's how it works

Once you have connected your Kindle device to a wireless network and then registered it with an Amazon account, the final step is to configure your payment details.

You need to do this on a computer by logging into the Amazon website and then delving into your account settings to set up the 1-Click Payment Method. You enter your preferred credit card details and a shipping/invoice address, then you can purchase books and other digital literature on your Kindle device within seconds by clicking the 'Buy' button. This is useful for making quick purchases but also dangerous if you are

prone to impulse buying! Thankfully, there is a way to avoid being out of pocket in the event of unintentionally clicking 'Buy'.

In this tutorial we'll guide you through the process of setting up your 1-Click Payment Method on your computer. We will also take a look at the confirmation screen that is displayed when you make a purchase through your Kindle, which is good to be familiar with because if you happen to accidentally purchase a book that you only intended to look at – easily done with the quick and easy payment method – then there is a way to cancel your purchase and get your money refunded.

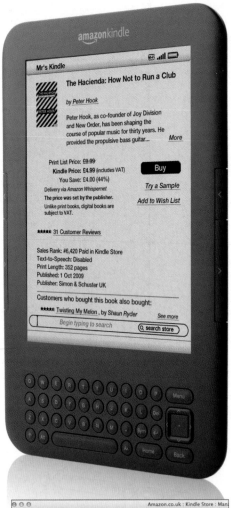

"You can purchase books on your Kindle device within seconds"

01: Go to the website

To start setting up your 1-Click Payment details, go to the Amazon website on your computer and then highlight the 'Kindle' option in the menu in the top-left corner. This will bring up a sub-menu; select 'Manage Your Kindle' from there.

02: Select payment settings

On the next page, all aspects of your Kindle account will be listed in columns down the left-hand side of the screen. Under the 'Your Kindle Account' section, click on the 'Kindle Payment Settings' option.

Buying books with 1-Click

Once your Amazon account has been set up, buying books is easy

Cancel order
If you have second thoughts then you can click on the 'Purchased by Accident?' link to delete the download and refund your money

Instant search
You can start searching for other books as soon as you have made a purchase. The confirmation screen has a built-in search bar so you don't waste any time

AUTOMATIC BACKUP
All Kindle purchases from the Kindle Store are automatically backed-up online at Amazon and available through your Archived Items on your Kindle or online at the 'Manage Your Kindle' page. You can re-download content wirelessly for free at any time.

Your purchase
Once you have clicked the 'Buy' button, your purchase will be sent to your device and will appear on your Home screen within a matter of seconds

Return to Store
Once you have seen your delivery message, you can then click on the 'Return to Store' link to continue browsing and buying other items

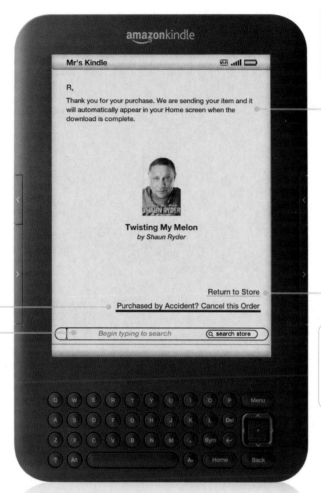

03: Edit details
On the next screen, under your 'Default 1-Click Payment Method' section, will be the option to 'Edit' your payment details. Click on this and then select your payment type and enter all relevant details and then click 'Continue'.

04: Shipping address
Enter your invoice address or, if already an existing Amazon customer, choose an address that you have already stored in your account and then click 'Continue'. Your 1-Click Payment Method has now been set up.

Kindle Store

Search over 1 million books in the world's biggest eBook marketplace

40
■ Access all these categories and more as you navigate the Kindle Store

54
■ Newspapers are just one of many things you can buy in the Kindle Store

1
UPMINSTER KID

"My mum got the milk train down to Truro because they told her I wasn't going to make it. It was in Nissen huts, barrack huts, an RAF-type hospital, and they let her come to the outside, and they turned the light on over my bed – you know, she saw my little white face on the pillow: a four o'clock in the morning job. But I was still there the next morning."

– Ian Dury

"Good Evening, I'm-from Essex, in case you couldn't tell," Ian growls, prompting roars of approval from the audience. "My given name is Dickie, I come from Billericay, and I'm doing very well." A few jaunty notes on the piano and Ian Dury and The Blockheads carry their fans off on a carousel ride of music hall and Essex laddism, courtesy of one of Ian's best loved lyrical creations, 'Billericay Dickie'. From his earliest dalliance with rock'n'Roll through to his very last gigs, Ian became universally identified with his characteristic stage persona. Off stage, in interviews and conversation, he cultivated a roguish image and his

Page 60

■ *Buy an eBook from the Amazon website*

Page 66

■ *The Amazon website makes it easy to manage content*

Key pick
Page 46
Start your eBook collection now by buying your first book from the Store

44
■ *Download a sample and see if that book's the one for you before buying it*

"The Kindle Store is by far the most heaving marketplace for eBooks in the world"

Connect to the Kindle Store

The Kindle Store is where over 1 million books are ready and waiting for you, so let's get connected…

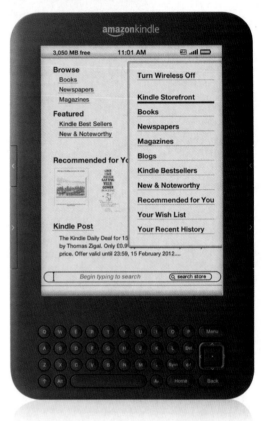

Naturally, the first thing you'll want to do with your new Kindle device is to get connected to the Kindle Store so that you can start searching for new reading material to peruse on it.

Before you can connect to the store, you first have to ensure that your Kindle is connected to a wireless network and registered to an Amazon account. We have guided you through the process of doing both earlier in this book, but for a quick heads-up, press the 'Menu' button while on your Home screen, then use the five-way controller to navigate down to the 'Settings' section. You can connect to the Kindle Store via the 'Menu' button and, once in, you'll be immersed in a thriving world of digital literature, where finding

and discovering exciting new eBooks is easy, and purchasing and downloading them to your device even easier. The literature is broken down into four simple categories – Books, Newspapers, Magazines and Blogs – and selecting a category will present you with specific sections that relate, so you can gradually narrow down your search for the books or other reading matter you're interested in.

With over 1 million digital books to download, the Kindle Store is by far the most heaving virtual marketplace for quality eBooks in the world. New releases are added every day, enabling you to shop and buy the most eagerly anticipated books on the day of release without having to leave the house – result!

"You'll be immersed in a thriving world of digital literature"

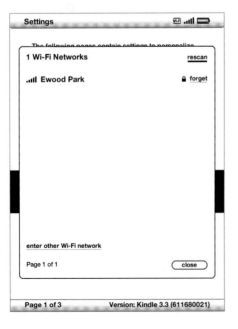

01: Connect to Wi-Fi
You'll need to connect to a wireless network to connect to the store. From your Home screen, press the 'Menu' button, use the five-way controller to navigate down to 'Settings', then click on 'Wi-Fi' settings and connect to an available network.

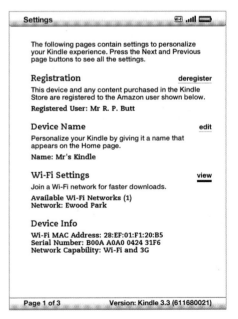

02: Register your Kindle
Still in 'Settings', use the five-way controller, navigate to the 'Register' option and then you will be presented with two main options – to log into an existing Amazon account or create a new one from your device. Choose one and register your device.

Getting connected to the store

Once you have met the prerequisites, it's time to start shopping

Time and space
When you press the 'Menu' button, the current time and available space will be displayed in the top bar of your Kindle's Home screen

Your content
All of your downloaded content will appear on your Home screen and you can sort and organise it from there, however you see fit

STORE MENU
If you press the 'Menu' button while in the Kindle Store you will bring up a new set of options that relate to the environment. These options allow you to jump straight to specific sections of the store or view your Wish List and Recent History.

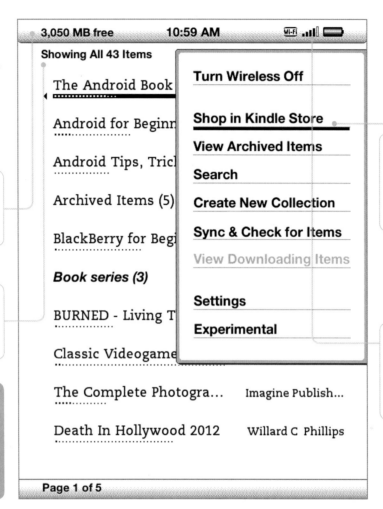

3,050 MB free   10:59 AM   Wi-Fi

Showing All 43 Items

The Android Book

Android for Beginn...

Android Tips, Tric...

Archived Items (5)

BlackBerry for Begi...

Book series (3)

BURNED - Living T...

Classic Videogame...

The Complete Photogra...   Imagine Publish...

Death In Hollywood 2012   Willard C Phillips

Page 1 of 5

Turn Wireless Off

Shop in Kindle Store

View Archived Items

Search

Create New Collection

Sync & Check for Items

View Downloading Items

Settings

Experimental

The menu
Pressing the 'Menu' button will present a list of options, the main one being 'Shop in Kindle Store'. Choose this to start purchasing new reading material

Wi-Fi connection
When you are connected to a Wi-Fi network a 'Wi-Fi' icon will be displayed on the top bar of your Home screen, indicating that you can connect to the store

03: Connect to store
Press the 'Back' button to return to the Home screen and then press the 'Menu' button. Now choose the option called 'Shop in Kindle Store' and your Kindle device will wirelessly connect to the store within a matter of seconds.

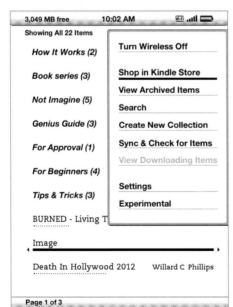

3,049 MB free   10:02 AM   Wi-Fi

Showing All 22 Items

How It Works (2)

Book series (3)

Not Imagine (5)

Genius Guide (3)

For Approval (1)

For Beginners (4)

Tips & Tricks (3)

BURNED - Living T...

Image

Death In Hollywood 2012   Willard C Phillips

Page 1 of 3

Turn Wireless Off

Shop in Kindle Store

View Archived Items

Search

Create New Collection

Sync & Check for Items

View Downloading Items

Settings

Experimental

04: Start browsing
The front page of the Kindle Store is uncluttered and user-friendly. To get started searching for new reading material, click on any of the categories under the 'Browse' header or start typing keywords to perform a search.

Mr's Kindle   Wi-Fi

Browse   amazon.co.uk

  Books   Blogs

  Newspapers

  Magazines

Featured

  Kindle Best Sellers

  New & Noteworthy

Recommended for You

See All

Kindle Post

The Kindle Daily Deal for 15 February is *The White League* by Thomas Zigal. Only £0.99, you save 79% off yesterday's price. Offer valid until 23:59, 15 February 2012....

Begin typing to search   🔍 search store

Navigate the Kindle storefront

When you first connect to the Kindle Store, it'll bombard you with options and categories. Let us guide you…

Visiting the Kindle Store for the first time can be exhilarating and slightly daunting. With so many options available it can be hard to know where to start browsing.

Your first port of call should be the top section, titled 'Browse'. This has four categories: Books, Newspapers, Magazines and Blogs. To search for books to download, use the five-way controller to navigate down to the 'Books' category (so that the block line appears under the title) and then click on it. An extensive list of sub-categories will then allow you to search through all of the books, which could take a while, or jump to a particular theme – such as Fiction, Business & Finance or Food & Drink. Browsing a themed

category will list every book that relates to it, which is good for whiling away a few hours seeing what's available. But if you are looking for something specific then a handy search bar is ever-present on every page, so you can enter keywords and author names to be warped straight to the digital e-literature you're after.

Also featured on the storefront are the current bestsellers (it's always good to know what's popular) and new releases – both are listed under the 'Featured' header, plus recommended reads, which are Amazon's suggestions based on your searches and purchases. It's a friendly, intuitive interface that is sure to point you to some great books that are tailored to your specific tastes.

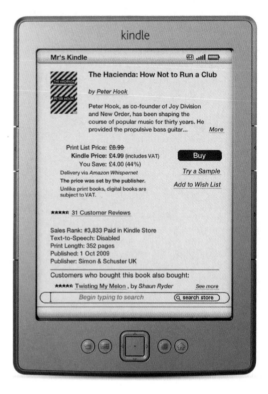

"The Kindle Store can be both exhilarating and slightly daunting"

01: Browse

The 'Browse' section lets you click on one of four categories – Books, Newspapers, Magazines and Blogs. Each category, when clicked on, will give you a complete rundown of all media for that category and let you browse by specific section.

02: Featured

The 'Featured' section shows the current bestsellers and newest releases in the Kindle Store. In the bestsellers list you can view books by paid or free categories, while the 'New and Noteworthy' option provides a list of the most notable new books.

Navigating the Kindle storefront

We guide you through the front page options on the Kindle Store

Latest and greatest
All of the latest releases will be showcased in the 'Featured' section along with the most popular digital publications that everyone is downloading and reading

Search
If you are looking for a particular book or author then you can enter keywords into the search engine and your device will scan the entire store for possibilities

---

Mr's Kindle   Wi-Fi .ııll ▭

 **amazon.co.uk**

Browse
   Books   Blogs
   Newspapers
   Magazines

Featured
   Kindle Best Sellers
   New & Noteworthy

Recommended for You

      See All

Kindle Post

The Kindle Daily Deal for February 8 is *Sektion 20* by Paul Dowswell. Only £0.99, you save 78% off yesterday's price. Offer valid until 23:59, February 8, 2012....

[I]   *Begin typing to search*   (Q search store)

Browse categories
If you just want to explore the store then click on either the Books, Newspapers, Magazines or Blogs categories to peruse the media available in those sections

Recommendations
Amazon takes note of what you search for and buy and will suggest books of a similar ilk that may be of interest to you. You can view the extensive list here

CATCH A BLOG
As well as digital books, newspapers and magazines, the Store has an expansive range of blogs that cover a wide range of topics. All of these blogs are free to read.

03: Recommended for you

This section provides quick links to the books that may be of interest to you based on previous searches and purchases. This is a good way to discover books you may otherwise be unaware of that are tailored to your likes and interests.

04: Kindle Post

This is an interesting news section that regularly features in-depth interviews with particular authors who provide detailed insight into what inspired their books. It's something to get your teeth into and enjoy for free.

Search the Kindle Store

Ready to start searching for exciting new digital reading material in the Kindle Store? Then let us show you how

Unlike the Kindle Store on the Amazon website – which is rammed full of sections, options and links – the Kindle Store, when browsed through your Kindle device, is a more friendly place that is perfect for looking for new reading material.

When you first access the Store, everything is neatly arranged, making it easier for you to start searching. If you're after a book but don't know what, you can simply select the 'Books' category and choose a theme, such as 'Crime, Thrillers & Mystery' to narrow down

your search. Or if you want to see what's hot or what's new, the 'Featured' section is the perfect place to go. The Kindle Store even carefully notes down what you buy and what you search for and will recommend books based on your particular likes – a nice touch.

01: Browsing
The four basic categories of reading material in the Kindle Store – Books, Newspapers, Magazines and Blogs – will be listed at the top of the storefront. Use the five-way controller to navigate to and select one of these four options to be taken to that specific category.

02: Featured material
If you want to see what books are popular with other people and the hottest new additions to the store then you'll find options under the 'Featured' section. When browsing the bestsellers you can filter your search to see the top 100 free books as well.

03: Recommended for you
The store will remember and take note of your previous purchases and searches and recommend other books that relate. This is a good way to discover new books that you may not have been aware of that are tailored to suit your tastes.

04: Searching
Start typing text on a Kindle keyboard and this text will be automatically placed into the search field for you to find specific books and authors. If using a standard Kindle 4 device, press the Keyboard button and then use the five-way controller to select letters.

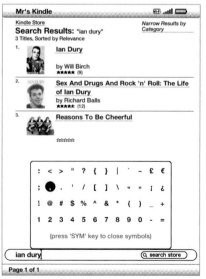

Browse New & Noteworthy and Best Sellers

How to discover all of the exciting new releases and find out what's hot on the Kindle Store

If you're not sure what you're looking for, the 'Featured' section is the place to go. It has two options: Best Sellers and New & Noteworthy. Best Sellers is a great place to discover what other Kindle users are buying.

You can filter your searches here by organising the content in various categories and even view the Kindle Top 100 Free books.

The New & Noteworthy section is where all of the latest releases are added. So if you're eagerly awaiting the release of a new book, you'll find it here first and can buy it straight away without having to search for it in other sections. In this tutorial we guide you through the 'Featured' section in full.

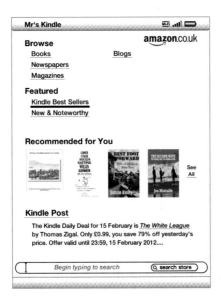

01: Navigate to 'Featured'
The storefront of the Kindle Store features several main categories, one of which is 'Featured', which includes the two sub-sections – 'Kindle Best Sellers' and 'News & Noteworthy'. Navigate down and select one of these using the five-way controller.

02: Best Sellers
The Best Sellers section lists the top 100 paid-for books by default. Use the Next Page or Previous Page buttons to scroll through the various pages. You can also use the five-way controller to select the 'Kindle Top 100 Free' section at the top of the page.

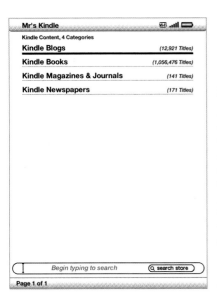

03: Filter by category
While on either of the Top 100 pages (paid for or free), use the five-way controller to select 'View These Best Sellers by Category' at the top and you'll be able to break the content down into the four main categories: Blogs, Books, Magazines and Newspapers.

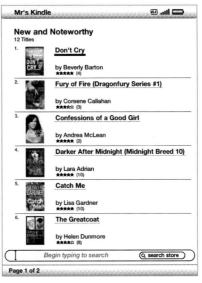

04: New & Noteworthy
Content that has just been added to the Kindle Store will appear within the 'New & Noteworthy' section under 'Featured'. Here you can use the five-way controller to scroll down to each book and click on it to bring up the specific information page for it.

Download and read a book sample

If you're unsure that the book you're searching for is right for you, try before you buy by downloading a sample

We respect authors for the time and effort they put into writing books, but the fact of the matter is that not all of them are good. Some books you hear about as being absolute stonkers, but nothing rings true as loudly as your own opinion, so what better way to determine if a book you're looking at is the right one for you than downloading and reading a sample?

Downloading a free sample is a service that is offered for any book in the Kindle Store, and doing so is incredibly easy. When searching for books, you will undoubtedly end up at a particular book's info page, which provides useful info such as the price, blurb and various other facts. Also on this page,

beneath the price is a link to 'Try a Sample'. If you navigate to this using the five-way controller and then select it, a free sample will be instantly downloaded and transferred wirelessly to your device, and within seconds it will be visible on your home screen.

Once downloaded, you can click on the extract and open it up on your device, whereby you'll be able to read a decent chunk so as to get a feel for the book and determine if it is one you would like to read further, in which case you can either select the 'Buy Now' option when you get to the end of the sample or delete it from your device and forget you ever had the misfortune of sampling it.

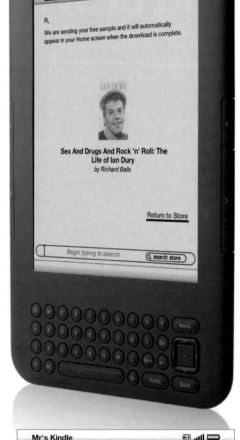

"Downloading a free sample is a service that is offered for any book"

01: Go to the Kindle Store

From the home screen, press the 'Menu' button and use the five-way controller to scroll down to 'Shop in Kindle Store'. If you are connected to a wireless network, this will take you to the Kindle storefront.

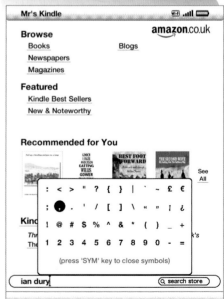

02: Find a book

Click on 'Books' in the 'Browse' section and find a particular book you are interested in, or start typing keywords like the title or author into the search field. This can be done by typing on a Kindle Keyboard or pressing the 'Keyboard' button.

Book info pages

Free samples is just one of many options a book's info page provides…

Book info
Clicking on a book will take you to its info page. Here, you can view the full title and author, read a blurb that details what the book is about and see how much it costs

Buying a book
If you like what you see and are happy to proceed with a purchase, then click on 'Buy' and use the one-click payment method to download the book to your Kindle

Try a sample
To try before you buy and download a free sample of the book, click on the 'Try a Sample' option to get an extract sent to your device

Add to Wish List
The Kindle Store allows you to make lists of books you would like to receive as gifts. If relatives and loved ones need inspiration then you can forward them your list

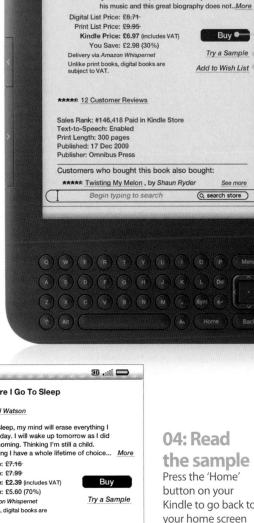

DELETING SAMPLES
Once you have read a book sample, you can delete it from your device by highlighting it on your Home screen and then pressing the left arrow on the five-way controller. This will call up the 'Delete' option, so select this and it will be instantly deleted from your library.

03: Go to book page
When you find a book that you like the look of, click on it to go to its info page. Then, under the 'Buy' option, will be a link called 'Try a Sample'. This will download a free sample to your home screen, where you will receive a message of confirmation.

04: Read the sample
Press the 'Home' button on your Kindle to go back to your home screen and sort your content 'By Most Recent First'. Locate and select your sample (the word 'Sample' will be visible next to the title) then click on it to open it up and read it.

The bedroom is strange. Unfamiliar. I don't know where I am, how I came to be here. I don't know how I'm going to get home.

I have spent the night here. I was woken by a woman's voice – at first I thought she was in bed with me, but then realized she was reading the news and I was hearing a radio alarm – and when I opened my eyes I found myself here. In this room I don't recognize.

My eyes adjust and I look around in the near dark. A dressing gown hangs off the back of the wardrobe door – suitable for a woman, but someone much older than I am – and some dark-coloured trousers are folded neatly over the back of a chair at the dressing table, but I can make out little else. The alarm clock looks complicated, but I find a button and manage to silence it.

It is then that I hear a juddering intake of breath behind me and realize I am not alone. I turn round. I see an expanse of skin and dark hair, flecked with white. A man. He has his left arm outside the covers and there is a gold band on the third finger of the hand. I suppress a groan. So this one is not only old and grey, I think, but also married. Not only have I screwed a married man, but I have done so in what I am guessing is his home, in the bed he must usually share with his wife. I lie back to gather myself. I ought to be ashamed.

I wonder where the wife is. Do I need to worry about her arriving back at any moment? I imagine her standing on the other side of the room, screaming, calling me a slut. A medusa. A mass of snakes. I wonder how I will defend

14%

Purchase a book

Buying books through your device is easy and can be set up to take place with a single click. Here's how it works

Purchasing, downloading and reading books is essentially what your Kindle is all about, so it's time to get down to business and buy your first digital eBook through your device. This is an easy process, made all the more simple thanks to the one-click payment method. Search the store until you find something you like, and click the 'Buy' button to complete the purchase.

The transaction takes place in seconds, and within a minute your book will be digitally delivered to your home screen, whereby you'll be able to get to grips with the intuitive interface of your Kindle device. In this tutorial, we guide you through the simple process of buying your first book from the Amazon Store, something you'll no doubt be doing a lot of in the subsequent weeks and months.

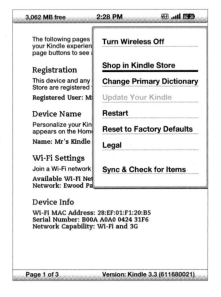

01: Head to the store

From your Kindle Home screen, press the Menu button and use the five-way controller to navigate down to the 'Shop in Kindle Store' option. You will then be transported to the Kindle shop front, where you can start browsing for goods.

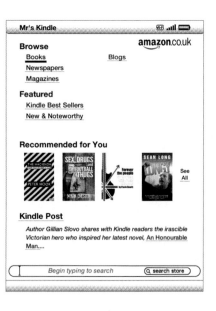

02: Search for items

The front of the store will be full of sections and recommendations, including books, newspapers and magazines, as well as the 'Recommended for You' selection, which will throw up books based on previous searches.

03: Browse an item

When you find a publication that takes your fancy, use the five-way controller to navigate to it, and click on the cover to bring up a page of info, including a brief overview and the price. To go ahead with the purchase, click on 'Buy'.

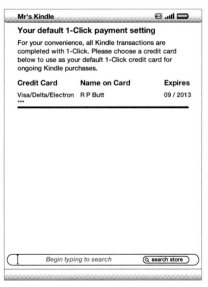

04: Your one-click payment

All that's left now is for you to confirm your payment and credit card details, which you will only have to do once when using the Kindle for the very first time, and your intended purchase will be delivered direct to your device within seconds.

Name your Kindle

It's a minor feature, but a cute one – we show you how to christen your device with its own name that appears on the home screen

Kindles enable you to read a wealth of digital literature in a natural and engaging way, but beyond that the basic features are somewhat limited. However, you can personalise your device by giving it its own name. Once you have christened your Kindle, it'll be visible on your home screen, and, once your device has been registered, on the Amazon website when you're managing your device online.

Naming your device is easy, as there is a section dedicated to it in the Settings screen, which is accessible from your home screen by pressing the 'Menu' button. Once you have carried out the fundamental set-ups needed to get your Kindle connected to a network and registered to an Amazon account, go ahead and give it a name to be proud of.

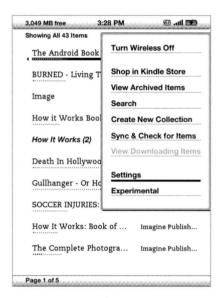

01: Go to Settings

From your device's home screen, press the Menu button. This will call up a list of options, one of which is called 'Settings', so use the five-way controller to navigate your way down to it, and select it by pressing the middle button.

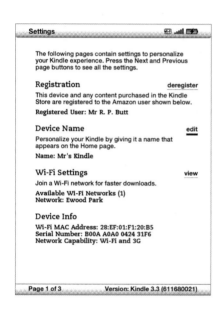

02: Select Device Name

Once you're in the main Settings screen you will see a section called 'Device Name'. Navigate your way down to this using the controller, and then highlight the 'Edit' link that is next to it before selecting it using the middle button.

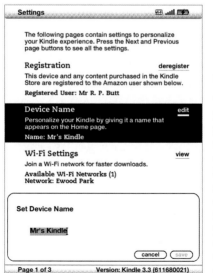

03: Name your Kindle

Now, using the integrated keyboard of the Kindle Keyboard, or by pressing the Keyboard button on a standard Kindle device, enter a suitable name for your device. Once you have finished entering text, click on the 'Save' option to store the name.

04: See the name

Once you have saved the name for your device, it will be visible on your home screen in the top-left corner and be visible online when you access the Kindle Store through the **Amazon.com** or **Amazon.co.uk** website, which is a nice touch.

Add books to your Wish List

If you see a book that you really, really want but can't afford, why not add it to your own personal Wish List?

The Wish List has been a feature of the Amazon website stretching back for as long as we can remember. It's essentially a list that you can add products to, as you search and encounter them on the site, which can then be emailed to friends and family. The idea being that whenever you think of an item that you want, you can add it to your list and then not have to rack your brains thinking of stuff you want when put on the spot as Christmas or your birthday rapidly approaches. This feature is, naturally, extended to the Kindle Store, so when browsing for books, any that you don't buy on the spot can be added to your own personal Wish List for you to refer back to later or circulate to your nearest and dearest so that they may buy you something that you really, really want.

01: Browse the store
From your Home screen, press the Menu button and choose the Shop in Kindle Store option. The four basic categories of reading material are Books, Newspapers, Magazines and Blogs – start with books and find something you like.

02: Click on the book
When you come across a book you like the look of, click on it to call up its info page and then on the right of the page you will see three options – Buy, Try a Sample and Add to Wish List. Choose the latter option to stick the item on your list.

03: Get confirmed
You will receive a message of confirmation that your item has been added to your list. To view items that have been added to your list, press the Menu button while in the store and then navigate down to the Your Wish List link.

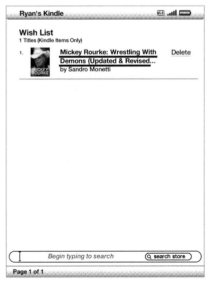

04: Your Wish List
You can manage your Wish List from your Kindle device by deleting items, but you can also sync it to your Amazon account and from the website. Click on the Wish List option at the top of the page and then you can share it via email, Facebook or Twitter.

Return an item

Is there any way back if you buy a book in error or find that you aren't completely satisfied with your purchase? Yes, and we show you the way

We're only human and sometimes we make errors with our purchases. Heck, Amazon's 1-Click Payment method is so quick and easy that you may accidentally buy something – and be aware that once you click Buy, there is no further confirmation you need to enter to rubber-stamp your purchase. But all is not lost. If you do purchase a book by mistake then on the screen that confirms your purchase, you will see a Purchased by Accident? option at the bottom – if you choose this option then your order will be cancelled, the money refunded to your account and the book will instantly vanish from your Kindle. You can also return unwanted books, so if you aren't happy with your purchases then there are avenues you can go down to reclaim your cash.

01: Cancelling an order

If you buy an item in error from your Kindle device then, straight after pressing the 'Buy' button, you will see a screen confirming your order. At the bottom is a 'Purchased by Accident?' link – click this to cancel the order and get all your money refunded.

02: Managing your account

If you wish to return a book at a later date, log on to the **Amazon.com** or **Amazon.co.uk** website and then, under the Shop All Departments menu in the top-left corner, go to the Kindle section and choose 'Manage Your Kindle'.

03: Your Library

All of the items that you have downloaded and transferred to your Kindle device will be listed in the main window and next to each item will be an Actions drop-down menu. Click on an item you have purchased and then choose Return for Refund.

04: Return for Refund

A new window will then appear in which you must confirm that you would like to return the item. Select a reason for your return from the drop-down menu provided and then click the Return for Refund button. The offending item will be removed and all your money returned to you.

Navigate the Kindle Store on Amazon

The web version of the Kindle Store is even more of a feature-rich beast

The Kindle Store is a bustling marketplace of enthralling e-literature, that much we know. But if you access the store through your internet browser then the experience is expanded ten-fold. What's also interesting is that the same recommendations that are suggested on the storefront on your Kindle device are also present on the webpage – which is proof enough that the store you browse on your Kindle is the same one that you access online through your computer.

In truth though, the storefront on the web presents many more options, many more categories and many more links. So while the store that you can access through your Kindle device is simple and functional for browsing and downloading digital literature, shopping online through your web browser is a more enlightening way to discover what's out there.

The Browse section, presented in a column down the left-hand side of the screen, is huge and covers all topics, from buying Kindle devices and apps to getting help with your device and, oh, the small matter of browsing through all of the various Book, Newspaper and Magazine sections available in the store.

All of the many sections are also listed in the main window, along with cover images of the current best sellers, and columns down the right-hand side provide links to the various accessories available for your Kindle device and the best-seller charts for paid-for and free books. In this tutorial we guide you around the Amazon web store and pick out the particular places of interest.

Amazon's online storefront
Finding your way around the packed front page

Kindles for all occasions
If you're browsing the online store and you don't own a Kindle, then you can buy one here. You can also download Kindle reading apps for a multitude of different platforms, including iPad, Windows and Android

Start searching
If you are looking for a particular book or works by a particular author then you can enter keywords into the search bar at the top of the page. You can also use the drop-down menu to define the area you wish to search, in this case, the Kindle Store

Get some help
The site features extensive tutorials and FAQs to help you get started and manage your device. Here you can set up your 1-Click Payment method and learn what the various buttons on your device do – handy if you have inherited a Kindle

Main sections
All of the key sections will be listed in the main window, such as recommendations, books, newspapers and magazines. The Browse column on the left-hand side of the screen will also help you search these categories in more detail

01: Access the Kindle Store

You will see a list in the top-left corner under the Shop All Departments banner. Click on the Kindle link and then choose Kindle Store. This will take you to the digital e-literature wing of the store.

02: Sub-sections

The webpage is a lot more in-depth, starting with the Browse section. Here you can get help with all aspects of your device, as well as extensive sections dedicated to specific media and themes.

03: Browse genres

If you scroll down the page you'll come to the Kindle Books section, which presents the various genres available. If you click on a genre, then you'll see a list of thousands of books.

04: Grab a newspaper

Scroll further down the main page and you'll see a section dedicated to Kindle-compatible newspapers. You can download one under the no-obligation trial and try it out for two weeks.

05: Read a magazine

The next section on the main storefront is dedicated to magazines. Click on the 'All Kindle Magazines' link to browse all Kindle-compatible magazines available for your device.

06: Pre-orders

The final section on the main storefront screen is dedicated to all of the books that are coming soon. If you're eagerly anticipating the release of a particular book then you can pre-order it here.

Explore books through the Amazon website

We take a look at all of your options when you browse for a new book on the Kindle Store

In this guide we are focusing on the Books section of the Kindle Store, which you can access from the main Amazon home page by clicking on the Kindle section of the Shop All Departments menu and then selecting the Kindle Store option.

Book categories are selectable from the main window of the Kindle Store page under the Kindle Books heading. If you scroll down the Browse menu in the column to the left of the screen, then you will find a section called Kindle Books under which is listed every category of book that you could ever think of, as well as a handy link called All Kindle Books.

Once you're at the main Books page, all of the categories of books will be listed in the column down the left-hand side. If you favour a particular type of book over another then you can select a category from here to narrow down your search considerably. If you aren't sure of which books are worth reading then the Amazon customer reviews are a good indication. Books are awarded an average score out of five based on user reviews, so the more stars a book is awarded, the better.

As you will see, there is plenty to discover in the Kindle Store's Book section.

"Books are awarded an average score out of five based on user reviews"

01: Browsing by category

The main window of the Books section presents a list of books with applicable info such as title, author, price and average review score. If you click Sort By, then you can organise them by various categories.

02: Department links

Listed down the left-hand column are the various book categories with the number of books available for that particular category. You can use these links to jump to the type of books you're interested in.

Navigating the Book department

We guide you through the Books section of the Kindle Store

Search

If you are looking for a particular book or author then you can enter keywords into the search engine and Amazon will scan the entire store for possibilities

Sort by

When you access the Books section, the main window will display the most popular books by default, but you can use the 'Sort by' drop-down menu to arrange them by price or release date if you prefer

Book categories

All of the various categories of books will be available for selection from the list in the left-hand column. The number of books available for each category will be presented in brackets

Reader reviews

More often than not, each book comes with a rating out of five, which is based on the average score awarded to the book by other Amazon users. It's handy for making an informed choice on what to buy

CATCH A GLIMPSE

Clicking on individual books will bring up specific info pages. By clicking on the cover of the books, you can also take a peek inside the book to read a sample of the text. If you like it, select the 'Buy now with 1-Click' option.

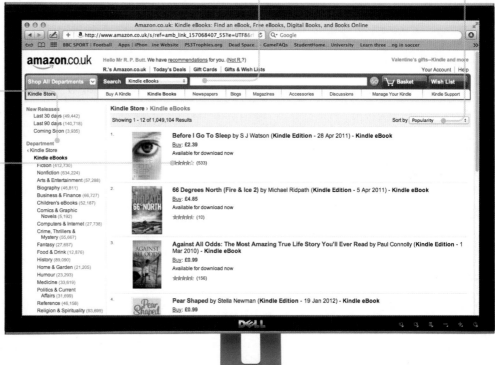

03: Coming soon

You will see a section called New Releases at the top of the left-hand column. You can use these links to browse books released in the last 30 days, 90 days or preview books that are coming soon.

04: Customer reviews

The last section in the left-hand column allows you to browse for books based on the scores awarded by other Amazon users. This is a decent way to gauge which books are worth reading.

Explore newspapers through the Amazon website

If you're into daily newspapers and want to find some informative reading material for your Kindle, take a tour of Amazon's virtual news rack

Where the newspaper section of the Kindle Store that you view through your device is formatted quite conservatively for ease of navigation, the same section on the Amazon website is quite different.

There are many more sections and categories packed with links and ways to discover new digital daily news publications. In this guide we are focusing on the Newspaper section of the Kindle Store, which you can access from the main Amazon home page by clicking on the Kindle section of the Shop All Departments menu and then selecting the Kindle Store option.

The most popular newspapers are selectable from the main window of the Kindle Store page under the Kindle Newspapers: Start Your 14-Day Free Trial Today heading, but if you scroll down the Browse menu in the column to the left of the screen then you will find a section called Kindle Newspapers, under which is listed the main territories that the available newspapers are applicable to, as well as a link called All Kindle Newspapers – click on this to get to

the main dedicated newspaper section. Like with Kindle magazines, all digital newspapers are available on a 14-day free trial, so although you initially have to make the arrangements necessary to set up a subscription, you don't pay anything for the privilege of

downloading newspapers during the two-week period. Reading newspapers this way is an environmentally sound way forward, although it does leave you the problem of finding something else to line your kitty litter trays with.

01: Scroll down to Newspapers

On the main Kindle Store window, scroll down and you will come to a section called Kindle Newspapers. The most popular ones are displayed or you can click on 'See more in Kindle Newspapers'.

02: Popular dailies

The 48 biggest sellers are selectable from the window in the middle of the page, and several of these will be flagged up lower down the page for you to click on and read more about.

Navigating the Newspaper department

We guide you through the Newspaper section of the Kindle Store

Free trials
All Kindle newspapers come with a 14-day free trial. You can download and read the papers daily during this trial period before you have to pay out any cash for the privilege

All Newspapers
Click on the 'All Kindle Newspapers' link in the left column or the 'See more in Kindle Newspapers' link in the main window – you'll be taken to the dedicated newspaper section

Quick links
The column to the left of the screen will allow you to click on countries that are applicable to the newspapers available. Kindle newspapers are currently available for the Asian, European and North and South American territories

Kindle Newspapers
Scroll down the main storefront window and you'll come to the 'Kindle Newspapers' section, where you can quickly scroll through 16 of the most popular digital dailies using the arrow icons. Click on a cover to go straight to that newspaper's page

CUSTOMER REVIEWS
By accessing a particular title's page, you can read customer reviews by scrolling down to the bottom of the page. These provide a well-rounded opinion on how good the publication is and how well it has been formatted to Kindle.

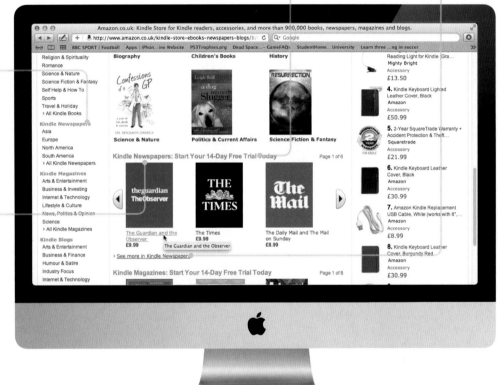

03: View all newspapers
Click on 'Browse our entire Kindle Newspaper selection' at the top of the page and the main window will display all of the newspapers available. Click the 'Sort by' menu to arrange the list by preference.

04: Buying newspapers
Click on a newspaper to go to its dedicated page. Here you can buy individual copies or subscribe using the 1-Click method. All newspapers also feature a 14-day free trial.

Kindle Store

Explore Kindle magazines from the Amazon website

If you're into monthly magazines and want to find some fresh reading material for your Kindle, we take a look at how you can get your favourite magazines digitally

Searching for magazines on the Amazon website is quite different than doing it directly from your Kindle device, as there are many more sections and sub-sections packed with intriguing links and ways to discover new digital publications.

In this guide we are focusing on the Magazine section of the Kindle Store, which you can access in the same way as with Newspapers (see page 54) by entering the Kindle Store from the main home page and browsing the list on the left-hand side of the screen.

Popular titles are shown in the main screen on the Kindle Store under the Kindle Magazines: Start Your 14-Day Free Trial Today heading, which is a great way to start browsing for options. If you want to see more, then scroll down the Browse column to the left of the screen until you get to the section called Kindle Magazines. Here you can either select a specific category, or you can opt to view all the titles in one list, which you can sort how you wish. If you aren't sure of which magazines are worth reading then the Amazon customer reviews are a

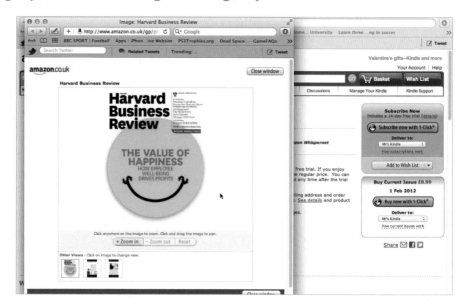

good indication. Magazines, like books, are awarded an average score out of five based on submitted user reviews, so the more stars a magazine is awarded, the better it promises to be.

Although there are only around 150 magazines available for Kindle at present, the market is growing all the time, so keep coming back to see if your favourite print publications have made the transition to Kindle.

01: Enter the magazine store

In the left-hand menu, scroll down to Kindle Magazines, and then click 'See more in Kindle Magazines' to go to the dedicated magazine department.

02: Most-read titles

The next page is peppered with the most popular digital magazines. You can immediately see the biggest sellers in this window, which you can click on to view more information.

Navigating the Magazine department

It's easy to find fresh reading material for your Kindle

Free trials

All Kindle magazines come with a 14-day free trial, so you can try before you actually pay anything. When subscribing you have access to the latest issues and can opt out of paying out for the subscription; otherwise, do nothing and your account will be debited

Categories

If you know what kind of title you want, use the categories here to narrow your search with options like Art & Entertainment and Science. This enables you to jump straight to the topics that interest you, narrowing your search options in the process

Kindle Magazines

You can find the Kindle Magazines section from the main Kindle Store using the left-hand Browse column. Click on a cover to go straight to that magazine's page

BUYING HABITS

When you click on a particular magazine's page then a useful list will display what other Amazon users have bought after viewing that magazine's page. This can be a good way to discover books and other magazines you may not have otherwise been aware of.

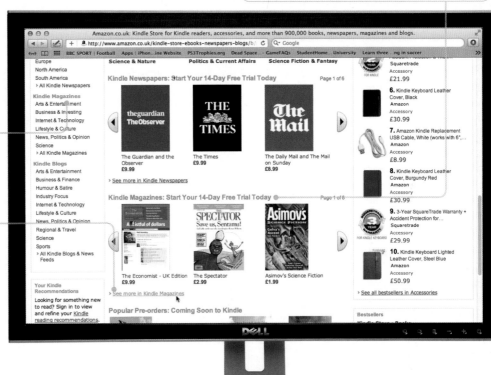

03: View all digital mags

Click on the 'Browse our entire Kindle Magazine selection' link to be able to see an entire list of the magazines currently available. Use the 'Sort by' menu to arrange the list how you want.

04: Buying magazines

Click on a magazine that you are interested in to go to its main page. You can buy a one-off issue or subscribe using the 1-Click option. You can get a free 14-day trial to any magazine.

Explore blogs and news feeds on the Amazon website

If you want something enthralling and informative to dip into on your Kindle, then blogs make for perfect coffee-break reading. Here we provide the full lowdown

As well as books, magazines and newspapers, your Kindle device is also good for reading pretty much anything, including blogs and news feeds. These are great, insightful reads that you can dip into whenever the fancy takes you and the range on offer covers a vast range of topics to suit all interests.

In this guide we are focusing on the Blogs and News Feeds section of the Kindle Store, which you can access from the main Amazon home page by clicking on the Kindle section of the Shop All Departments menu and then selecting the Kindle Store option from the drop-down menu.

The blog market is significantly smaller than the books, magazines and newspapers departments, and this is reflected by the amount of real estate the section takes up on the main Kindle Store page. None of the main window is dedicated to blogs, so to find the section you have to scroll down to the bottom of the Browse column on the left-hand side of the screen. You can start by choosing an area of interest directly from the column or you can click on the All Kindle

Blogs & News Feeds link at the bottom of the list to head to the general department.

A lot of blogs are free, but others you will have to pay a subscription for. However, like with Kindle magazines and newspapers, all digital blogs are available on a 14-day free trial, so although you initially have to make

the arrangements necessary to set up a subscription, you don't pay anything for the privilege of downloading blogs during the two-week period and can opt out of your subscription when the trial ends. Read on to discover how to find a blog that's right for you.

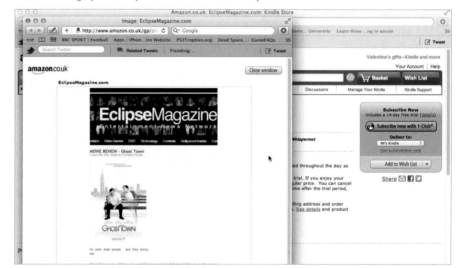

01: Scroll down to Kindle Blogs

On the main Kindle Store window, scroll down and you will come to a section called Kindle Blogs at the bottom of the Browse column. You can jump to a specific category here or click the 'All…' link.

02: Popular blogs

The next page consists mainly of a list that presents all 12,000+ available blogs and news feeds. They are listed by most popular by default, but sort them however you want with the 'Sort by' menu.

Browsing the blog department

We guide you through Blog section of the Kindle Store

Info page

After browsing through the various categories of blogs and news feeds, if you click on one you like the look of then you'll be taken through the main info page where you can read all about the content that it delivers and perhaps make a purchase

Product details

Scroll down the page and you can read a full product description to help determine if the blog is something you would like to subscribe to, and also read reviews by fellow Amazon customers to ascertain if it is any good

SPECIAL DELIVERY

Any items that you purchase through the Amazon website can be delivered directly to your Kindle device, as long as it has been registered to your Amazon account. Use the drop-down menu under the 'Buy/Subscribe with 1-Click' button and choose your device. Once purchased, it will appear on your device's Home screen.

Add to wish list

If you're shopping for blogs, or any other items and subscriptions for that matter, that you would like but don't necessarily want to buy yourself, you can click the Add to Wish List button so that the item is stored for others to see and perhaps buy as a gift for you

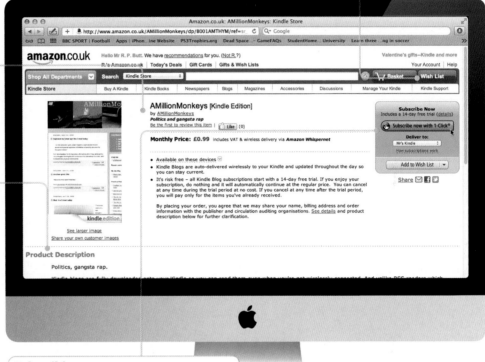

Subscribing

If you like what you see from the product description, you can click on the 'Subscribe now with 1-Click' button. Like the magazines and newspapers, blogs and news feeds come with a 14-day free trial so you can sample them without shelling out

03: Exploring blogs

The left-hand column allows you to search by particular categories. Clink on a link, for example Arts & Entertainment, and you'll then be presented with a list of sub-categories for that topic.

04: Buying blogs

When you find a blog of interest, click on it to go to its page and you can get a full description and details, customer reviews and more. Click on the 'Subscribe now with 1-Click' button to buy it.

Purchase from the Kindle Store on the Amazon website

Buying items from the Kindle Store is easy and what's more, your items can be beamed straight to your device wirelessly

There are a few advantages of shopping online at the Kindle Store and purchasing items through your web browser. However good and intuitive your Kindle device is, there's no substitute for a big screen and a mouse. This is probably why the web-based Kindle Store is a buzzing hive of activity in stark contrast to the streamlined, more conservative format that appears on your Kindle. If you are under any reservations that buying digital literature on your computer and transferring it to your Kindle is in any way fiddly then we're here to dispel your fears.

Referring to our earlier tutorials, you will now be aware of how to connect your Kindle device to a Wi-Fi network and how to register your device to an Amazon account. Once those two simple tasks have been completed then any purchases you make online through the website will be beamed straight to your device and will be waiting on your Home screen the next time you turn it on. The process occurs over something called the Amazon Whispernet, which is Amazon's fancy

name for the transferral of files wirelessly over a Wi-Fi or 3G network.

To make purchases through the Kindle Store website, all you have to do is find a product that you want to buy, click on the 'Buy now

with 1-Click' button and then the magic happens. All you have to be wary of is that if you press the button in error then there is no instant cancellation process like there is on your Kindle – so watch what you click on.

01: Find an item

Browse through the Kindle Store's extensive range of books, magazines, newspapers and blogs and when you see an item you would like to buy, click on it to go to that particular item's main page.

02: Purchase the item

Now ensure that your registered Kindle device is selected in the 'Deliver to' drop-down menu in the top-right corner of the screen, and then click on the 'Buy now with 1-Click' button.

Making a purchase
We guide you through the process
of buying an item

Buying the item
If you have set up your 1-Click payment details then you can buy items quickly and easily by clicking on the 'Buy now with 1-Click' button. Once done, the item will be instantly sent straight to your Kindle device wirelessly

Add to wish list
Amazon Wish Lists are handy because you can add items to them from all over the store and invite friends and family to view them and pick items from the list to buy you as presents

Info page
After browsing through the various categories of blogs and news feeds, if you click on one you like the look of then you'll be taken through the main info page where you can read all about the content that it delivers before making a purchase

Deliver to…
If you have registered your Kindle device with your Amazon account then click on this drop-down menu and choose your device from the menu to ensure that your purchase gets delivered straight to your Kindle after purchase

TRY BEFORE YOU BUY
If you want to read an extract from the book before committing to the purchase then click on the 'Send Sample Now' button to get a few sample pages sent wirelessly to your device so that you can read them and determine if the book is the one for you.

03: Confirmation of purchase
You will now receive a message that your item has been purchased and will be auto-delivered to your Kindle wirelessly via Amazon Whispernet.

04: Auto delivery
Within seconds, your purchase will be wirelessly transferred to your Kindle device. When you next switch on your Kindle, your new purchase will be visible at the top of the main Home screen.

Receive your Kindle Store purchases from Amazon

There are different ways in which content purchased from the Amazon website can be relayed to your Kindle device

Once you have purchased a book or other item from the Amazon.com or Amazon.co.uk website, there are two ways in which you can receive your purchases – automatically or manually. You will receive your purchase automatically without you having to lift a finger as long as you have connected your Kindle to a Wi-Fi network and registered your device with the Amazon account that you are using to purchase the item through the website. You will perform these two actions when initially setting up your Kindle device (and we guide you through the process earlier in this book), making it a quick and easy process to purchase and download items from the Kindle Store directly on your device or via the webpage.

If you do buy from the webpage, simply because you find it simpler and more intuitive to browse the store on a computer and find what you want on a bigger screen packed with many more options than the Kindle-formatted Kindle Store page, then your purchased goods will be delivered straight to your device, without hassle or delay.

If, on the other hand, your Kindle isn't connected to a wireless network, then getting your goods to your device is still relatively painless. In this case you simply have to connect your device to your computer with the USB cable that comes supplied with it and then manually copy your downloaded digital literature to your Kindle by dragging it and copying it to the 'Documents' folder.

However your purchases are received, you're never more than a few minutes away from enjoying them on your Kindle reader. Like so many aspects of your device, receiving files is quick and easy, which is why Kindles are gradually taking over the world.

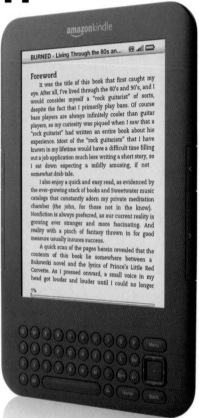

"It's a quick and easy process to purchase and download items"

01: Register your Kindle

To receive your purchased items automatically you must first connect your device to a Wi-Fi network and register your Kindle with an Amazon account. You can do this via your device or the website.

02: Receiving files

When you purchase items from the Kindle Store to a registered Kindle that is connected to a Wi-Fi network, the items will automatically appear at the top of your Kindle's Home screen within minutes of purchasing them.

Receiving files on your Home screen

We demonstrate where the new files appear when beamed to your Kindle

New files
Files that have recently been added to your Home screen will be marked with a 'New' flash next to the title to flag up the fact that it is a new addition to your list of digital literature

Turn pages
If your list of digital files extends further than a single page, you can switch pages by pressing the Next Page flipper button on the side of your device

MORE FLAGS
Different digital files will be flagged up in different ways on your Home screen. As well as being 'New', content is flagged up if it is a 'Sample' or 'Audio', so you can get an at-a-glance heads-up as to the type of content you are dealing with.

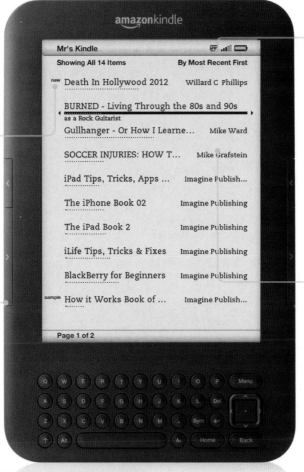

Your connection
Depending on how your Kindle device is connected to a network, an icon will be visible on the top bar that will state either 'Wi-Fi' or 'GPRS' (if you are connected via a 2G or 3G mobile network)

Your files
All of your purchased digital literature will be listed on your Kindle Home screen. You can determine the order of the list by clicking on the top option and picking how you want the list ordered

03: Manually copying files
If your Kindle device isn't connected to a Wi-Fi network, you can transfer purchases manually. Connect it to your computer via USB and drag the downloaded files into your Kindle's 'Documents' folder.

04: Happy reading
Through whatever means your purchased items are beamed to your Kindle, you're only ever a few minutes away from opening your digital literature and enjoying hours of prime reading through your device. Try it once and you'll never go back to paper again.

Bobby Driscoll (March 3, 1937 – (March, 1968) American child actor

Robert Cletus Driscoll was born in Cedar Rapids, Iowa in 1937. Bobby was the only child of an insulation salesman, and a schoolteacher. Soon after his birth, his family moved to Des Moines where they lived until 1943. When a doctor advised Bobby's father to relocate

1%

Purchase & transfer books without Wi-Fi

Don't have an active Wi-Fi network or 3G connection? Transfer your purchases to your device via USB

Kindles are versatile devices designed to enhance your reading experience, and they don't let the small matter of a lack of Wi-Fi or 3G network stop you from buying new things to read – because you can do it all through the Kindle Store section of the Amazon.com or Amazon.co.uk website, as we have demonstrated in previous tutorials.

Not being connected to a network isn't an issue, because you can use the USB cable that comes bundled with your Kindle device to connect it to your computer. When buying an item, select the 'Transfer via Computer' in the 'Deliver to' drop-down menu, and subsequently get the item downloaded to your machine. It is then just a simple case of opening up your Kindle device on your desktop and copying the downloaded file to the 'Documents' folder.

Once copied, the purchased files that you originally downloaded to your computer will now appear on your Kindle's Home screen, thus allowing you to get down to business reading them. With so many free Kindle apps available for so many different devices – including iPads, iPhones, Android devices and personal computers – there really is no excuse not to at least try reading digital literature.

As we have demonstrated here, there are numerous ways to get your purchased items to your Kindle device, making it by far the quickest and most convenient way of reading literature in the digital age. The only problem you will have is keeping tabs on your spending, because there is so much choice available on the Kindle Store that it's possible to bankrupt yourself in minutes if you're not careful!

01: Find an item

Browse the Kindle Store's extensive range of books, magazines, newspapers and blogs, and when you see an item you would like to buy, click on it to go to that particular item's main info page.

02: Purchase the item

Go to the 'Deliver to' drop-down menu in the top-right corner and select 'Transfer via Computer'. Ensure that the Kindle is connected to your computer via the USB cable, and tap 'Buy now with 1-Click'.

Transferring purchases via USB

We guide you through the process of manually moving your purchases

Deliver to...

If you are planning on manually transferring your purchased book files via USB then click the 'Deliver To' drop-down menu and then select the 'Transfer via Computer' option. You can also deliver it wirelessly or via 3G from this menu

Info page

After browsing through the various categories of blogs and news feeds, if you click on one you like the look of then you'll be taken through the main info page, where you can read all about the content that it delivers and perhaps make a purchase

How to buy

If you require a little additional info on how to buy books and transfer them to your Kindle device then click on the 'How buying works' link, which can be found under the 'Deliver to' option in the top-right corner

READ ON YOUR COMPUTER

The Kindle Store detects what type of computer you are using to access the site, and provides a link called 'Available on your Mac/PC'. If you click on this then you will be taken to a link to download the Kindle app for your computer.

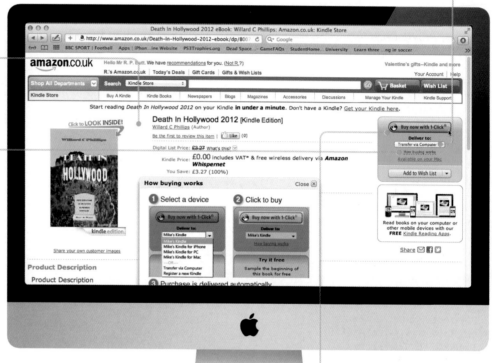

Buying the item

If you've set up your 1-Click payment details then you can buy items quickly and easily by clicking on the 'Buy now with 1-Click' button. Once done, the item will be sent in accordance to the method selected in the 'Deliver to' drop-down menu

03: Select your Kindle

You will then have to choose which Kindle you plan to transfer your purchase to via USB, so click on the 'Deliver To' drop-down option and select your device. Once done, click on the 'Continue' button.

04: Manual transfer

Your purchase will be downloaded to your computer, where a message will prompt you to save your file. Open your Kindle device on your desktop, then locate and copy it to the Documents folder.

Manage your Kindle Library Content

All of the items you purchase from the Kindle Store can be displayed and managed via the Amazon website. Here, we show you how

Thanks to Amazon, it is impossible to lose track of items that you have purchased through the Kindle Store. By clicking on the 'Manage Your Kindle' link at the top of the page or in the left-hand column, you can view all of the items that you have ever purchased across all categories of media, and choose specific actions to deal with them.

It may be that you've purchased items on your computer before you bought a Kindle device, in which case you can explore the various options for transferring those items to your device both wirelessly and via USB. Or perhaps you have bought an item in error and wish to apply for a refund, in which case click on the 'Actions' drop-down menu next to a specific item and pick an action accordingly.

In this section you can also register a Kindle device, adjust your payment settings, change your country and shipping address if you move, and set up your Personal Documents Settings so that you can transfer documents to read on your Kindle and have with you at all times without the need to physically print them out. Whatever you need to manage, you can do it all through the 'Manage Your Kindle' section. In this tutorial, we guide you around this section of the website…

"You can instantly view all of the items that you have ever purchased"

01: Manage your Kindle

From the Kindle Storefront, click 'Manage Your Kindle', which can be selected from the bar at the top of the page or via the 'Browse' column to the left of the screen under the 'Need Help?' section.

02: Your library

Log into your Amazon account if you haven't already, and the main screen will display the items that you have purchased from the store. To change the category, click on the 'View' drop-down menu.

Manage your Kindle library

We guide you through the process of managing your purchased items

Actions
You can manage specific items by clicking on the 'Actions' drop-down menu next to each item. Here, you can transfer items, apply for refunds or delete items from the list

Get help
If you require any additional help with managing your account or your device then you can click on the 'Kindle Help' link in the top-right corner of the screen

Your items
Your items can be viewed by particular categories, which you can specify by clicking on the 'View' drop-down menu then picking a category to display

Manage your account
You can manage all aspects of your account by clicking on an item under the 'Your Kindle Account' section in the left-hand column, such as set up Personal Documents

YOUR PERSONAL DOCUMENTS

Kindles are environmentally friendly, eradicating the use of paper. This includes the printing out of personal documents, as you can get those delivered to your Kindle. Select 'Personal Document Settings', and you can see how to retrieve documents emailed to your Kindle.

03: Managing your content

Each item in your library will have an 'Actions' drop-down menu next to it. You will be able to deliver the item wirelessly to a Kindle, download the item to your computer, transfer via USB or delete it.

04: Getting refunds

You can use the 'Actions' menu to apply for refunds. Select 'Return for Refund', and a separate window will appear. Select the reason for returning the item and click the 'Return for Refund' button.

Using your Kindle

Detailed step-by-step tutorials that explore the basics of reading on your Kindle device

Virals

professors.
My take? I just do what I do.
Piles of shells littered the kitchen table. Sundials. Shark's Eyes. Turkey Wings. Recently cleaned and buffed,

Aa Aa Aa Aa Aa Aa Aa Aa

Typeface   regular condensed sans serif

Line Spacing   small medium large

Words per Line   fewest fewer default

Text-to-Speech   turn off pause

Speech Rate   slower default faster

Speaking Voice   female male

Screen

2%

Page 80
■ Kindle Keyboards can read your books to you

Key pick
Page 82
Make the most digital bookmarks and never lose your place again

Key pick
Page 70
Get to grips with your first eBook with our guide to Kindle navigation

"The Kindle makes it easy for you to find your way around a book"

98
■ Collections are an integral part of a Kindle's interface

Hollin's Kindle

novels
2 Items

Open Collection
Add/Remove Items
Rename Collection
Delete Collection

BILL BRYSON

Edit Collection Name

novels

cancel   save

I ATE A SHARK

he didn't wait for
d or hugs from
r new T-shirt

aw Rocky
aring a
and a

74
■ Make full use of the Kindle's fantastic E-Ink display by zooming into pictures

Page 88
■ Define tricky words with the built-in dictionary

learn more about setting up your 1-Click payment method on your Manage Your Kindle page, go to www.kindle.com/support.

After you order, the Amazon Whispernet service delivers the item directly to your Kindle via

purchase v. [with obj.] 1 acquire (something) by paying for it; buy: Mr Gill spotted the manuscript at a local auction and purchased it for £1,500. ARCHAIC obtain or achieve ...
Press ⊙ for full definition, highlight, or note

Settings

Voice Guide   turn on
Navigate your Kindle with spoken menus, selectable items, and descriptions.

Send-to-Kindle E-mail
You can send documents to your Kindle by using the e-mail address below. To change your settings, go to: www.amazon.com/myk. For UK customers, go to: www.amazon.co.uk/myk.

Device Password   turn on
Restrict access to your Kindle by creating a password.

Device Time   set manually
Set the local time on your Kindle.

Social Networks   manage
Share notes and highlights with friends using your social network accounts (like Twitter or Facebook).

Popular Highlights   turn off

Set Time
5 : 42 pm

cancel   save

Page 2 of 3   Version: Kindle 3.3 (611680021)

Page 104
■ Who needs a watch when you've got a Kindle?

Access and navigate your eBooks

Finding your way around a Kindle eBook is easy thanks to the straightforward interface and navigation options

The Kindle aims to make it easy for you to find your way around a book. This is the core functionality of the device, and so it follows that there are a wealth of ways you can access the contents of your book. The first thing you'll need to do is get a book onto your Kindle – visit Amazon's Kindle Store or read our previous tutorials to do this simply and quickly. Once a book has downloaded onto your device, you'll see it appear on the home screen.

Use the five-way controller to navigate so that the book is highlighted, then simply click the centre button to open it. Once you're viewing a book, you can use the big previous and next page buttons along the side of your Kindle to move around between pages just as you would on a traditional book. There's a lot more than just being able to move through pages one at a time though!

Kindle allows you to jump directly to different chapters, the glossary or index (if applicable) and to search for specific phrases or words. This makes a Kindle book a whole lot more versatile and useful than a traditional paper one.

As you'll discover elsewhere in this book, you can also add notes, annotations and bookmarks throughout your eBooks, making the Kindle an ideal research tool too! Follow the tutorial below...

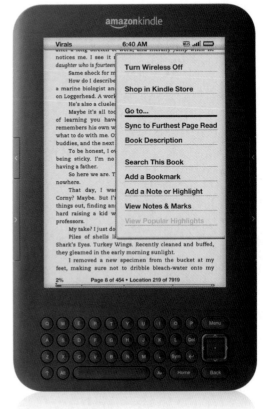

"A Kindle book is a whole lot more versatile than a paper one"

01: Find a book

Make sure you've got at least one book downloaded, then use the five-way controller to move around the home screen. The currently selected item is underlined. The number of dots shown beneath a title indicate its length, and the bold dots show your progress through that particular book.

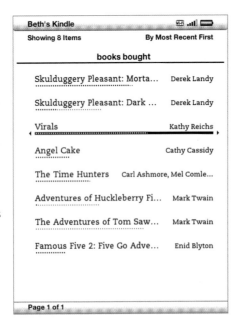

02: Choose a book

When you've got your book selected you can click the right button on the five-way controller to view the book cover art, and some useful navigation hyperlinks including 'Go to Page...'. Select Continue Reading to carry on where you left off, or skip by simply clicking the centre button on the five-way controller when you've highlighted the book in step 1.

Useful navigation

A look at the book details screen

Beth's Kindle `Wi-Fi` `.ıllll` `▭`

Virals
Kathy Reichs

Add to Collection...

Go to Last Page Read

Go to Beginning

Go to Page...

Book Description

Search This Book

Notes & Marks

Remove from Device

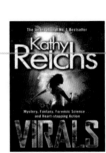

Go to...
There are several different Go To options when you're reading the book, accessed by pressing the menu button and choosing Go To. Here you can quickly browse to the last read page, the first page or a specific page of your choice

Add to Collection
Click this link to add the book to a collection. Think of this as a folder into which you can put as many books as you like to keep them organised. You can have as many different collections as you need!

Search this book
You can search for a specific phrase by choosing Search This Book. Kindle will take you to your last read page, and open the search bar. Type in your search and select Find to browse results

FIND OUT MORE
When you're viewing a book on your home screen, it can be difficult to remember what a book is about just from the title. Highlight the book with the five-way controller, then click the right arrow to view the summary. Choose 'Book Description' to view a summary of the book, complete with user reviews, on the Amazon Kindle store.

Remove from device
Select this option to delete the book. Removing a book doesn't throw it away altogether. Deleted books are added to the Archived Collection section

03: Move between pages
Moving between pages is really easy! Press one of the Previous Page or Next Page buttons along the side of the screen to move to the following or previous page as appropriate. The top button moves you to the previous page, the bottom – bigger – button takes you to the next one!

after a long stretch of work, and literally jump when he notices me. I see it register: *That's my daughter. I have a daughter who is fourteen and lives with me. I'm her father.*

Same shock for me, Pops. I'm working through it, too.

How do I describe my newfound dad? Kit is thirty-one, a marine biologist and research professor at the institute on Loggerhead. A workaholic.

He's also a clueless parent.

Maybe it's all too new—you know, the astonishment of learning you have a half-grown kid. Or maybe Kit remembers his own wild youth. In any case, he has no idea what to do with me. One day he chats me up like one of his buddies, and the next he treats me like a child.

To be honest, I own my share of the blame for things being sticky. I'm no saint. And I'm just as lost about having a father.

So here we are. Together. Smack dab in the middle of nowhere.

That day, I was classifying seashells by species. Corny? Maybe. But I'm a science nut. I live for figuring things out, finding answers. Mom always joked that it was hard raising a kid who was smarter than most college professors.

My take? I just do what I do.

Piles of shells littered the kitchen table. Sundials. Shark's Eyes. Turkey Wings. Recently cleaned and buffed, they gleamed in the early morning sunlight.

I removed a new specimen from the bucket at my feet, making sure not to dribble bleach-water onto my

2%

04: Navigate through your book
While reading your book you can press the menu button at any time to bring up a floating panel that gives quick access to the Go to panel. Highlight the words Go to and select with the centre of the five-way controller. You can now quickly and easily jump to a different section.

Virals `Wi-Fi` `.ıllll` `▭`

after a long stretch of work, and literally jump when he notices me. I see it register: *That's my daughter. I have a daughter who is fourteen and lives with me. I'm her father.*

Same shock for me, Pops. I'm working through it, too.

How do I describe my newfound dad? Kit is thirty-one, a marine biologist and research professor at the institute on Loggerhead. A workaholic.

He's also a clueless parent.

Maybe it's all too new—you know, the astonishment of learning you have a half-grown kid. Or maybe Kit remembers his own wild youth. In any case, he has no idea what to do with me. One day he chats me up like one of his buddies, and the next he treats me like a child.

To be honest, I own my share of the blame for things being sticky. I'm no saint. And I'm just as lost about having a father.

So here we are. Together. Smack dab in the middle of nowhere.

That day, I was classifying seashells by species. Corny? Maybe. But I'm a science nut. I live for figuring

Go to...

| table of contents | beginning | page |
| cover | end | location |

2%   Page 8 of 454 • Location 219 of 7919

Customise display settings

One of the best features of owning a Kindle is the ability to tailor the reading experience to suit your own preferences.

If you've ever suffered the indignation of having to reach for your spectacles to be able to decipher the printed word, you'll really appreciate the ability to set your Kindle up to meet your own preferences when it comes to contrast, text-size, screen rotation and words-per-line. As all the books in Kindle's catalogue are paginated automatically by the device, you can have as many or as few words per page as you like, allowing you to increase the font size if you find it easier to read larger type, change the font itself (which is especially helpful to users who will need a high contrast letterform) and the number of words per line.

Of course, if you like cramming as much information as possible onto each and every page then Kindle's got you covered here too – it's perfectly possible to go the other way and squeeze extra words onto the page!

There are eight different font sizes you can choose from, and several different font styles – so everyone will be able to find their own favourite. Do note, however, that the font size of the menus and other screens is fixed and can't be altered – so you'll need to be comfortable navigating around the device regardless of how large you make the text of your books.

Once you've set up the size and font for your Kindle, every book you read will use these settings until you change them again. This means you don't have to go into the menu system for each and every book.

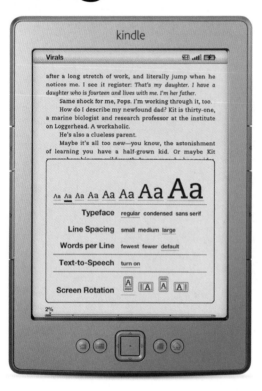

"You can have as many or as few words per page as you like"

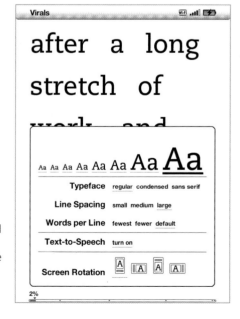

01: Open the display options
Press the Text key on your Kindle if you have a Kindle Keyboard, or if you have a Kindle without a keyboard press the Menu button, and choose the Change Font Size option from the pop-up menu.

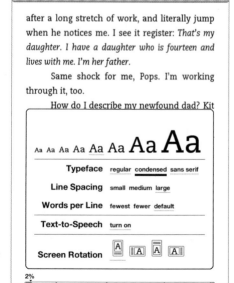

02: Choose your size
The Kindle allows you to select from eight different font sizes. As you move the five-way controller along the options, the text of your book behind changes so you can see a preview of the effect your changes will have.

Setting your font

Control how your book looks

KINDLE KEYS

The Kindle Keyboard has a dedicated Text key that opens the font settings box. Kindle 4s don't have this key so, when viewing a book, you have to click the Menu button and scroll up to the Change Font Size option.

Line spacing

Generally speaking, the greater the line spacing, the easier a passage of text is to read – but you need to balance this against the number of lines shown per page

Words per line

Shorter line lengths make it easier to track from one line to the next, so if you're struggling to find the beginning of the next line, try shortening the line length

---

Virals

after a long stretch of work, and literally jump when he notices me. I see it register: *That's my daughter. I have a daughter who is fourteen and lives with me. I'm her father.*

Same shock for me, Pops. I'm working through it, too.

How do I describe my newfound dad? Kit is thirty-one, a marine biologist and research

Aa Aa Aa Aa Aa Aa Aa **Aa**

Typeface	regular condensed sans serif
Line Spacing	small medium large
Words per Line	fewest fewer default
Text-to-Speech	turn on
Screen Rotation	

2%

Font Size

It's easy to select and preview different font size options from the choice of eight offered. Simply move your cursor over your preferred option using the five-way controller

Typeface

Not exactly different fonts in the sense of a word processor, but each option available on the Kindle offers a different letterform and shape. Experiment to find the one you're most comfortable with

---

03: Select your typeface

Choose your typeface, line-spacing and words per line in a similar manner to how you selected the font size. Please note that words-per-line doesn't space the words out more, it just reduces the column width to make for easier tracking of lines.

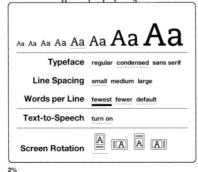

04: Choose your orientation

You can view content on your Kindle in any orientation: portrait, landscape, portrait upside down, and landscape upside down. Simply highlight your preferred option and click the button in the middle of the five-way controller.

Virals

2%

after a long stretch of work, and literally jump when he notices me. I see it register: *That's my daughter. I have a daughter who is fourteen and lives with me. I'm her father.*

Same shock for me, Pops. I'm working through it, too.

How do I describe my newfound dad? Kit is thirty-one, a marine biologist and research professor at the institute on Loggerhead. A workaholic.

He's also a clueless parent.

Maybe it's all too new—you know, the astonishment of learning you have a half-grown kid. Or maybe Kit remembers his own wild youth. In any case, he has no idea what to do with me. One day he chats me up like one of his buddies, and the next he treats me like a child.

To be honest, I own my share of the blame for things

Adjust font and image sizes

Use the on-screen menus and keyboard controls to adjust the text and picture sizes

The Kindle has an excellent range of default settings that help make the device so easy to pick up and read. It's worth noting, however, that if you'd rather shake things up a bit you don't have to stick with the recommended settings. There are a few extra tricks and tweaks tucked away within the menus that can be easily accessed with a few button presses.

These settings allow the user to make adjustments to the size of the text or add more spacing between lines. It's also possible to change the number of words that appear on each line. There are even a few extra fonts to try out, which is ideal for when the regular font becomes a little tired on the eyes. For books that contain pictures, the Kindle also offers some basic zoom functionality for viewing images. This very simple process will expand the picture to fill the screen and remove any text from view.

01: Font size menu

While reading a book, press the Menu button and use the five-way controller to select Change Font Size. For Kindles with a built-in keyboard the font size menu can be accessed by pressing the Text key (between Space and Home).

02: Adjust the settings

The Font menu provides the settings for font size, Typeface, Words per Line and Line Spacing. Simply move the cursor around each option and the Kindle display will automatically update the book text to give you a preview.

03: Zooming in on pictures

Some book titles include pictures. The Kindle makes it possible to zoom in on these images without having the text get in the way. To zoom in on a picture, position the cursor over the picture using the five-way controller.

04: Full-screen pictures

Once the cursor is over the picture a magnifying glass will appear on the image. Press down on the five-way controller to zoom in on the picture. When you're finished, press the five-way controller again to return to the book.

Search your books

If you're looking for a particular section of a book, the Kindle's built-in Search function can help

The Kindle presents a number of features that simply aren't possible with traditional books. One of the standout examples is the Search function that is built into the device. By using simple search terms, much like you would on Google or Bing, it's possible to jump straight to a passage of text of any book that is stored on a Kindle device. It's a function that proves incredibly useful for revisiting favourite parts of a novel.

The practicality of the Search function really comes into its own when the Kindle is being used for studying textbooks or referencing material. Rather than having to scan through the contents or index sections, you can instead open the Search function and go straight to the relevant pages with just a few button presses. The Search function can be used to search a single title or across your entire collection. In the tutorial we'll look at searching within a particular book.

01: Starting a search

When reading a book, press the Menu key and select Search This Book. This will open up the search box. Keyboard Kindle users can skip this step by using the keyboard; doing this will bring up the search box automatically.

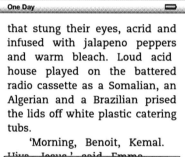
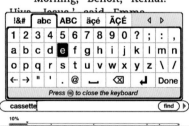

02: Enter your text

For non-keyboard users, press the keyboard button to start typing. Once you've entered your search words, press the keyboard button again to go back to the search box. Keyboard Kindle users can access punctuation marks by pressing the Symbol key.

03: Click to find

Once the search terms are entered, they will appear in the search box. Use the navigational pad to move the cursor over the 'find' button and select it. The Kindle will now search for all available instances of that phrase.

04: See the results

Once the search has finished, the display shows a list of each instance that it has found. Every result includes the page number and location. Using the five-way pad to select an entry will take you to that particular page.

Navigate to a specific location

Moving through content is one area in which a traditional method can't be beaten. Or can it?

Finding your way around a book on Kindle is pretty straightforward, especially if you want to go one page at a time. Knowing how to jump to specific locations within a book, however, will make your reading experience all the more enjoyable.

One of the best things about a traditional paper book is how easy it is to navigate around, as you're hopefully already aware. You can open it from either end, move backwards and forwards through it a page at a time, leap to a specific page number and so on. You may think that the Kindle is limited to moving through content one page at a time, but there's a wealth of navigation options that mirror everything you can do with a paperback – and more!

The 'Go To' function, found by pressing the Menu when you're reading a book, offers a variety of options, including the ability to jump to the start, the end, the table of contents (a list of chapters), or a specific page or location. Add to that the ability to jump directly to one of your unlimited bookmarks, and you've got a fantastic set of navigation tools!

Pages are relative on Kindle. As you can increase the size of the text, and the amount of space between lines, pages are reformatted accordingly. As a result, the 'page' metaphor as an absolute destination doesn't apply to Kindle; on Kindle, the location number is absolute, and linked to the content rather than the page number. In the future we'll all be saying "turn to location 343" instead of page 343!

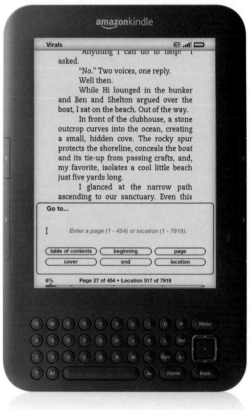

"Jump from section to section with ease on your Kindle!"

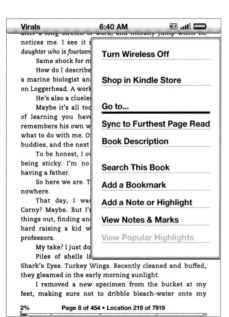

01: Open a book

Select a book from your home screen and start reading it! When you want to jump to another part of the book, press the Menu button and move your cursor down to the 'Go To' option in the menu that pops up.

02: Choose an option

From the resultant floating box, you can use the five-way controller to select a specific button. There are options for the table of contents, the start, the end and the cover. Each of these will work just by selecting the button and pressing the centre button on the controller.

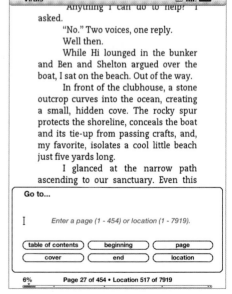

Advanced navigation

A quick look at the navigation options on a Kindle

Pop-up floating navigation box
The navigation pop-up allows you quick and easy access to the common parts of the book – the cover, table of contents, beginning and end are all preset options

Jump to page or location
If you know where you'd like to go, enter a page number or location number using the on-screen number keyboard, then select the appropriate button to complete your jump to the new area!

THE CHAPTER LINKS
Most books found on Kindle have a list of chapters at the start of the book. One quick way to jump around inside a book is to go to the start of the book, move to the chapter list and use it to navigate directly to the start of the desired chapter.

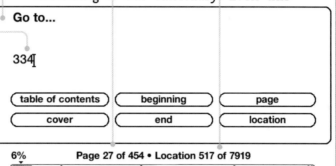

Where am I?
The Kindle shows you where you are in the current book, allowing you to see how many pages and locations there are. This is useful for getting a feel of the size of a book

Page numbers are relative!
Remember that page numbers will change as you increase the font size, line spacing and alter the line width. To note an absolute location within a Kindle book, quote the location instead of the page

03: Specify a page or location
To specify a particular page or location to jump to, you need to type in the number of the page or location to jump to. On the Kindle Keyboard you can access the numerical input by pressing the 'Sym' button. On a Kindle without a keyboard you'll have to ensure your on-screen keyboard is active first!

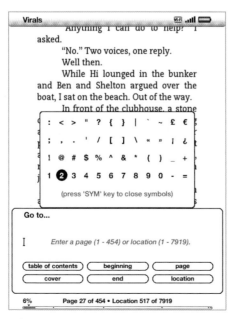

04: Finishing off
Once you've entered the number of the page or location, move your five-way controller to the appropriate button according to whether you entered a page number or a location number. Press the centre button on the controller to complete the jump!

Select links within a book

Navigate titles with ease using built-in hyperlinks throughout a book

A useful feature of Kindle titles is the links that are available within the text on the page. These can be identified as underlined sections of the text. These links work like the kind of shortcut links that you would find on the internet. Kindle-based links make navigating around a book title much easier, as different sections of a book can be accessed instantly. The most common example of this on a Kindle title is the table of contents. In most cases the table of contents will consist of a collection of links that relate to each section within the book itself. Using the five-way directional pad to select one of these links will take you to that section. This is a huge timesaver compared to manually flicking through each page one by one. Some titles may also include external links to the internet, although these can be dependent on your device settings and available data connection.

01: Identifying a link

The most common example of clickable links on the Kindle can be found within the contents section of a book. When a link is available on the page it will appear as a section of underlined text on the display.

> **TABLE OF CONTENTS**
>
> Welcome
>
> Chapter 1
> Getting Started with Your Kindle
>   Charging the battery
>   Using the controls
>   Status indicators
>   Setting up your Kindle
>   Special Offers & Sponsored Screensavers
>
> Chapter 2
> Acquiring & Managing Kindle books
>
> 1%

02: Selecting a link

When a link is available it can be selected via the cursor. Using the five-way directional pad, move the cursor to where the link is located. When the cursor is over the link it will change to a finger icon.

> **TABLE OF CONTENTS**
>
> Welcome
>
> Chapter 1
> Getting Started with Your Kindle
>   Charging the battery
>   Using the controls
>   Status indicators
>   Setting up your Kindle
>   Special Offers & Sponsored Screensavers
>
> Chapter 2
> Acquiring & Managing Kindle
>
> use v. [with obj.] 1 take, hold, or deploy (something) as a means of accomplishing or achieving something; employ: she used her key to open the front door | the poem uses ...
> Press ⊙ for full definition, follow the link or create note

03: Follow it through

When the link is selected, a menu will appear at the bottom of the display. The option to follow the link will be highlighted by default. By pressing down on the five-way pad the Kindle will follow the selected link.

> **TABLE OF CONTENTS**
>
> Welcome
>
> Chapter 1
> Getting Started with Your Kindle
>   Charging the battery
>   Using the controls
>   Status indicators
>   Setting up your Kindle
>   Special Offers & Sponsored Screensavers
>
> Chapter 2
> Acquiring & Managing Kindle books
>
> (cancel) (create note) (full definition) (follow link)

04: Going back again

The Kindle will now display the content at the other end of the link. To go back to the original page press the back button on the device. Depending on your settings, your book may also contain external web links.

> **Using the controls**
>
> You need to learn only a few simple controls to navigate around your Kindle to download and read books, magazines, and newspapers.

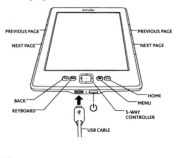

> PREVIOUS PAGE — PREVIOUS PAGE
> NEXT PAGE — NEXT PAGE
> BACK — HOME
> KEYBOARD — MENU
> — 5-WAY CONTROLLER
> USB CABLE
> 11%

Sync to Furthest Page Read

When reading the same book on multiple devices it's possible to sync the current page position

As well as the device itself, Amazon has also developed a Kindle app that is available for a range of popular platforms such as the iPad, iPhone and Android handsets. With Kindle being available on various formats, Amazon has included additional sync capabilities that work across multiple platforms. A very useful feature is Sync to Furthest Page Read. When a book title is read on one device, the latest page being read is also updated on any other devices that are connected to the same Kindle account. This process is made possible thanks to Whispersync, a feature of Kindle that runs in the background. Whispersync is an online network that connects your Kindle to your Amazon account and manages your content, personal settings and account information. By default Whispersync is activated on your account, but it can also be easily de-activated should you wish.

01: What is Whispersync?

Whispersync is a feature that syncs your Kindle usage with Amazon and across all Kindle-enabled devices. By default it is set to On. Should you wish to deactivate WhisperSync, it can be done via the Amazon website.

> Amazon's Whispersync technology keeps track of your last reading location in each book. For example, you can read a few pages using the Kindle application on your iPhone, iPad, or Android device and then pick up right where you left off when you return to your Kindle. To learn more about supported devices, go to www.kindle.com/support.
>
> **Sharing comments via social networks**
>
> You can share your Kindle notes and highlights with friends using
>
> 58%

02: Syncing to the right page

When it comes to syncing to your furthest page you needn't do anything. The Kindle will update the information automatically as you progress through a book. Syncing is dependent on having an active data connection.

> 1,313 MB free   02:05
>
> Showing 10 Items
>
> Kindle User's Guid | **Turn Wireless On**
> Judy Moody | **Shop in Kindle Store**
> Oxford Dictionary | Change Font Size
> One Day | **View Archived Items**
> Welcome Sonya | **Search**
> One Story | **Create New Collection**
> Henry Burp - Mind | **Sync & Check for Items**
> The Armchair Det | View Downloading Items
> The Armchair Det | **Settings**
> | **Experimental**
> The New Oxford A | **Screen Rotation**
>
> Page 1 of 2

03: Update your position

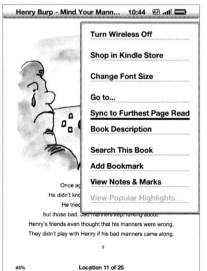

If you've read a title on another Kindle platform, it may not immediately update the page position the next time you open it on your Kindle device. When in the book, press Menu and select Sync to Furthest Page Read.

> Henry Burp - Mind Your Mann...   10:44
>
> Turn Wireless Off
> Shop in Kindle Store
> Change Font Size
> Go to...
> Sync to Furthest Page Read
> Book Description
> Search This Book
> Add Bookmark
> View Notes & Marks
> View Popular Highlights
>
> Once ag
> He didn't kno
> He tried
> but those bad, bad manners kept turning about.
> Henry's friends even thought that his manners were wrong.
> They didn't play with Henry if his bad manners came along.
>
> 8
>
> 43%   Location 11 of 25

04: Why deactivate Whispersync?

When sharing books on separate Kindle devices with the same account it can become tricky. In this example Whispersync may need to be switched off via the Amazon website.

> MonkeyPad Edit
>
> Device Synchronization (Whispersync Settings)
> With device synchronization on, your Kindle and Kind read. Synchronization will also keep track of any bool view them on another device.
>
> Whispersync Device Synchronization
>
> ON for S   A
>
> You should turn synchronization off only if:
> • You and someone else are reading the same b
> • The Kindles are registered to a single account
>
> Know Us | Make Money with Us
> s | Sell on Amazon
> r Relations | Associates Programme
> Releases | Fulfilment by Amazon
> n and Our Planet | Self-publish with Us
> | › See all

Use the Kindle Read Aloud function

Your Kindle Keyboard can read your book aloud automatically, so you can have books read to you!

Sometimes you need to get on with something other than reading, but can't bear to put your book down. Audiobooks, such as those from Audible (another company owned by Kindle-maker Amazon), offer a perfect solution, albeit at a cost.

The Kindle can happily store and play Audible files, so if you already have a collection of audiobooks in this format then you can easily copy them over to your Kindle and play them through headphones or the built-in speaker. A word of caution, however: the newer Kindle model without a keyboard doesn't have either a headphone jack or

speaker, meaning that it lacks the ability to play audio altogether.

So, assuming you have a Kindle Keyboard, you can happily listen to professionally recorded audio books, but what do you do if you're not keen on buying an audio version of a book as well as the Kindle version? Happily, your Kindle has a neat little trick up its sleeve that can solve this conundrum – it can read aloud to you from any Kindle book.

As with support for Audible content, this functionality isn't available on the newer Kindle without a keyboard, but if you have a Kindle Keyboard you can use the read-aloud feature either with or without headphones.

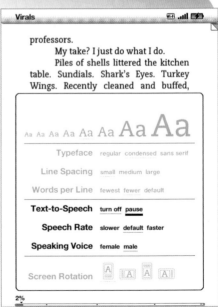

"If you have an audiobook collection you can easily copy it over"

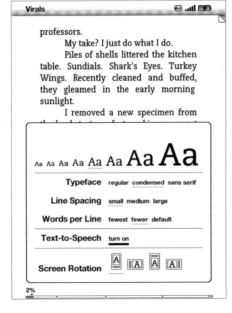

01: Turn on Read Aloud
To activate the Read Aloud function, start by opening a book. Once the book is open, press the 'Text' key to open the font and orientation options. If your Kindle is capable of text-to-speech, then the option will appear here – select it.

02: Play and pause
If you'd like to pause playback, press the Space key on your Kindle's keyboard. You can resume playback by pressing Space a second time. If you would like to turn off Text-to-Speech then press the Text button again and deselect the Text-to-Speech.

Text-to-Speech

Get your Kindle to read aloud to you

Speak to me!
When you're reading a book, press the Text button to open up the Kindle display properties panel. Choose Text-to-Speech from the options shown (note that you must have a capable Kindle to use this feature)

Change settings
Once you're listening to text-to-speech, press the Text button again to access special settings for the voice and speed of playback

READ ALOUD SHORTCUTS
The Kindle has a number of useful shortcut keys to quickly access common features. You can also play or stop Text-to-Speech by holding down the Shift key and pressing the Symbol key. You can pause and resume Text-to-Speech by pressing the spacebar.

Faster and slower
You can control the speed of playback, as well as the gender of the voice according to your personal preferences. Be aware that both of the options sound rather electronic!

Control playback
You can play and pause speech by pressing the spacebar on your Kindle's keyboard. You can also turn off speech by pressing the Text button and choosing 'Turn Off'

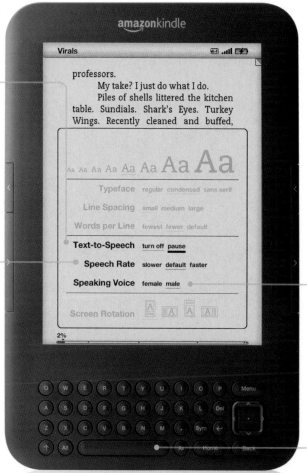

03: Change the voice
Once you're listening to playback, press the Text button to bring up the Text-to-Speech options. Choose between a male or female voice for the speech. The system default is male, but once you've set this it will become your default for future use.

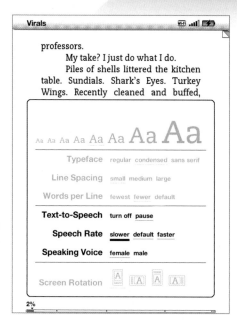

04: Change the speed
If you'd like to speed up or slow down the rate at which text is read aloud, then you're in luck. Press the Text button once Text-to-Speech is activated. A new panel will appear with Text-to-Speech options. Choose the appropriate option to either slow down or speed up the speech as desired.

Add bookmarks

Never find yourself stuffing a bit of junk mail in a book again. The Kindle offers bookmarking with extra goodies

Bookmarks are a vital part of enjoying a book over an extended period of time. They're useful not just for finding your place again, but they can often be found identifying useful passages or areas to share with others later. Of course in the paper-book world, anything smaller than your book will suffice as a bookmark, leading to creative use of unwanted mail in many a house!

On Kindle things are a lot better, and there's no need to retain all those bits of paper. Firstly, there's no need to specifically bookmark where you've got to in a particular book – Kindle will keep track of this automatically for you and reopen the book at the correct page the next time you come to view it. But bookmarks for

all the other scenarios are easier to create, keep track of and locate than a paper book could ever hope to achieve.

The Notes & Marks option, found in the menu when viewing a book (and on the book detail screen as you will see), offers a quick way to jump around between bookmarks, as well as preview highlighted passages and notes you'd added to your book. You can also use this function to quickly remove multiple bookmarks if you no longer wish to identify particular sections of the book.

Bookmarks are accessible from the home screen of your Kindle too, allowing you to quickly check a particular title for specific bookmarks without having to go into the book first. Read on to get up to speed…

"Bookmarks are a really useful way to find a section again later"

01: Make a bookmark

Adding a bookmark is really easy on Kindle. Simply navigate to the page you'd like to bookmark, then press the Menu button. From the pop-up menu that appears, select the Add a Bookmark option. Bookmarked pages have a dog ear in the top corner.

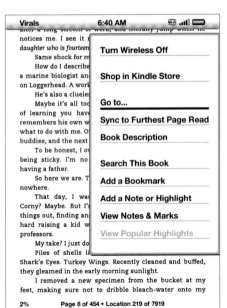

02: Place a bookmark

You can quickly place a bookmark by holding down the Alt key on your Kindle Keyboard, and pressing the 'B' key simultaneously. If you have a Kindle without a keyboard, press up on the five-way controller, then press the centre button twice quickly to place a bookmark.

Anatomy of a bookmark

An in-depth look at Bookmarks on Kindle

My Notes & Marks
The My Notes & Marks function on Kindle allows you to quickly see all the bookmarks you have placed in a particular book. This is a great way to get an overview of the book, as well as manage your bookmarks!

Add a bookmark
Add a bookmark quickly by holding down the Alt key on your Kindle and pressing the B key, or if you have a keyboardless model press up on the five-way controller then press the centre button twice in succession.

HOME SCREEN
You can quickly access your bookmarks for a specific book by selecting the book on the home screen of your Kindle and pressing the right button on the five-way controller. From the book details page select Notes & Marks to quickly access your bookmarks!

---

outer surface. Pleased with the rare find, I set it aside to dry.

Reach. Pull.

My next draw was a mystery. Ark? Cockle? Both clams are abundant on the South Carolina coast.

Despite having soaked in bleach for almost two hours, the shell's exterior was covered with caked-on debris. Barnacles and encrusted silt obscured all detail.

Excellent. I'd been looking for an excuse to use my power tools. They were a gift from my great-aunt Tempe.

You may have heard of her.

I was shocked when I found out. I'm related to Dr. Temperance Brennan, the world famous forensic anthropologist. She's kind of my idol. When Kit first told me, I didn't believe him, but his story checked out. Tempe's sister, Harry, is my grandmother.

So there's a celebrity in my

Begin typing to create a note or click to start a highlight

Recognising a bookmark
You can tell if a page has been bookmarked by looking at the top-right-hand corner of the screen. If you see a dog ear (a folded corner in the corner of the page) then the page has been successfully bookmarked!

Delete quickly
If you need to quickly remove a bookmark, select it from the My Notes & Marks area and press the Delete key. The bookmark will be removed immediately. You can repeat this with the remaining bookmarks as desired.

03: Remove bookmark
Getting rid of bookmarks is almost as easy as placing them! Navigate to the page with the bookmark you'd like to remove. Once there, press the Menu button and choose the Remove Bookmark option. The bookmark will be removed immediately.

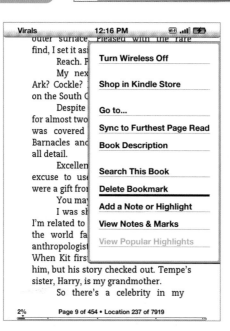

04: Quick removal
If you'd like to remove multiple bookmarks quickly, press the Menu button. From the pop-up menu, choose the My Notes & Marks option. Now select the bookmark you'd like to delete and press the Delete key. Continue selecting and deleting until all the bookmarks that you would like to remove are gone.

Highlight text

If you like to single out passages in a book, you'll love the Kindle's Highlight Text feature

There are many reasons why you might want to highlight passages in a book. Perhaps you're studying a text and want to be able to recognise important facts, dialogue or sections. Maybe you want to make a note of ingredients in a recipe, or you're learning lines from a play and want to show only the lines for your character. Whatever your motivation, the old-fashioned method of dragging a bright highlighter pen over the words has been transposed to the Kindle, and the digital version has numerous advantages over ink.

Highlighting passages on your Kindle is as simple as moving your cursor over the text you'd like to mark. A highlight is shown with an underline on the Kindle's screen,

but more importantly you can browse all your highlighted passages from one place, allowing you to quickly see the important passages in your book. You can create a single highlight that spans multiple pages too – making this feature flexible enough to cope with any scenario.

Once you've created your highlights you can view them by selecting the menu button and choosing My Notes & Marks. This menu option also provides the method for removing highlighted passages. As well as your own highlights, Amazon makes Popular highlights available so you can see what other readers have highlighted in a book – ideal for students examining a text or looking to bring out key learning points.

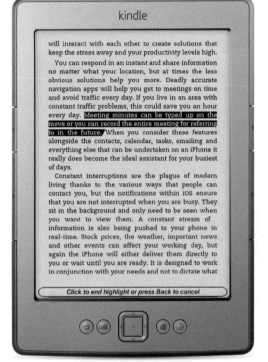

"The digital version of highlights has numerous advantages over ink"

01: Move your cursor
Use the five-way controller to move your cursor point to the start of the section you'd like to highlight. The cursor will only appear when you first press the five-way controller, so don't worry if you can't see it before you start.

> Begin typing to create a note or click to start a highlight
>
> ...fina, I set it aside to dry.
> Reach. Pull.
> My next draw was a mystery. Ark? Cockle? Both clams are abundant on the South Carolina coast.
> Despite having soaked in bleach for almost two hours, the shell's exterior was covered with caked-on debris. Barnacles and encrusted silt obscured all detail.
> Excellent. I'd been looking for an excuse to use my power tools. They were a gift from my great-aunt Tempe.
> You may have heard of her.
> I was shocked when I found out. I'm related to Dr. Temperance Brennan, the world famous forensic |anthropologist. She's kind of my idol. When Kit first told me, I didn't believe him, but his story checked out. Tempe's sister, Harry, is my grandmother.
> So there's a celebrity in my
>
> 2%

02: Anchor your start position
Once you've got your cursor at the start of the passage of text you'd like to highlight, press down the middle button in the five-way controller. This will anchor your starting point, ready for you to start selecting the text to be highlighted.

> Click to end highlight
>
> ...fina, I set it aside to dry.
> Reach. Pull.
> My next draw was a mystery. Ark? Cockle? Both clams are abundant on the South Carolina coast.
> Despite having soaked in bleach for almost two hours, the shell's exterior was covered with caked-on debris. Barnacles and encrusted silt obscured all detail.
> Excellent. I'd been looking for an excuse to use my power tools. They were a gift from my great-aunt Tempe.
> You may have heard of her.
> I was shocked when I found out. I'm related to Dr. Temperance Brennan, the world famous forensic anthropologist. She's kind of my idol. When Kit first told me, I didn't believe him, but his story checked out. Tempe's sister, Harry, is my grandmother.
> So there's a celebrity in my
>
> 2%

Highlighting a passage

Marking up important text for later reference

Delete existing highlights

Access and remove your existing highlights by pressing the Menu button and choosing My Notes & Marks. You can now select existing highlights and delete them by pressing the Del key

Highlight multiple passages

You can highlight multiple passages on a page, allowing you to pull out only the most important information to you. Individual highlights can be seen by pressing the Menu button and selecting My Notes & Marks

MANAGE POPULAR HIGHLIGHTS

You can turn off sharing of your highlights within the Popular Highlights feature by navigating to Settings on your Kindle and turning off Annotations Backup. Annotations Backup syncs your highlights across multiple devices, so consider whether that's important to you before turning this option off!

Click to end highlight or press Back to cancel

the page quicker to load and easier to navigate. This is ideal for grabbing short bursts of information – news headlines, sports scores, finding the answer to a crossword clue – rather than extended bouts of browsing, although you can do that too if you wish.

The different versions of the BlackBerry OS contain different versions of Browser. The Browser in BlackBerry 7, the latest version, is more powerful and feature rich than the older versions. While these versions are functional for most purposes, as you become a more experienced user you might want to download an alternative browser to power up your mobile internet experience.

Communication

If there is one area where BlackBerry truly excels, it is in communications. You won't find a better smartphone than this if staying in touch is what you want to do. The BlackBerry works like all other mobile phones for the basics. You can make calls, of course, as well as sending text and multimedia messages. But there are also two areas where it surpasses all of its rivals. The first of these is email. Other smartphones can do email, but none quite as efficiently as BlackBerry. The BlackBerry uses what is known as a 'push' email system. This means that instead of logging in at regular intervals, such as every 15

3%

Span multiple pages

Highlights aren't limited to a single page – if your text wraps over onto a second page simply press the previous page or next page buttons during the highlighting process to continue overleaf

Highlighted text

Highlighted text is shown with an underline while Popular Highlights, based on commonly highlighted passages, are shown with a dotted underline. You can choose whether to share your own highlights with the Popular Highlights service

---

03: Select the text

Move the five-way controller in either direction to start selecting text. You can also use the previous page and next page buttons to move across multiple pages with your selection. Continue moving your cursor until you've highlighted the entire passage you'd like to mark.

outer surface. Pleased with the rare find, I set it aside to dry.
　　Reach. Pull.
　　My next draw was a mystery. Ark? Cockle? Both clams are abundant on the South Carolina coast.
　　Despite having soaked in bleach for almost two hours, the shell's exterior was covered with caked-on debris. Barnacles and encrusted silt obscured all detail.
　　Excellent. I'd been looking for an excuse to use my power tools. They were a gift from my great-aunt Tempe.
　　You may have heard of her.
　　I was shocked when I found out. I'm related to Dr. Temperance Brennan, the world famous forensic anthropologist. She's kind of my idol. When Kit first told me, I didn't believe him, but his story checked out. Tempe's sister, Harry, is my grandmother.
　　So there's a celebrity in my

Begin typing to create a note or click to start a highlight

04: Complete the highlight

Once you've reached the end of the text you'd like to highlight, simply press the centre button of the five-way controller a second time to lock in your highlighted passage. You can add as many highlights as you'd like by repeating steps 2 to 4.

Virals

Showing All 3 Notes & Marks

Page 8 • Location 228　　Your Bookmark

saint. And I'm just as lost about having a father.
　　So here we are. Together. Smack dab in the middle of nowhere.
　　That day, I was classifying seashells

Page 9 • Location 237　　Your Bookmark

outer surface. Pleased with the rare find, I set it aside to dry.
　　Reach. Pull.
　　My next draw was a mystery. Ark? Cockle? Both clams are abundant on the

Page 9 • Location 245　　Your Highlight

anthropologist. She's kind of my idol. When Kit first told me, I didn't believe him, but his story checked out. Tempe's sister, Harry, is my grandmother.
　　So there's a celebrity in my family.

Page 1 of 1　　Close Notes & Marks

Add, edit and delete Notes

Your Kindle enables you to create, edit and delete notes – all without using a pen or damaging your book!

Kindles are great to read books on – they're light, portable and responsive, not to mention the fact that they come with the ability to carry an entire library without the device getting any heavier. But what you might not be aware of is that they also make fantastic research tools. Students will be familiar with the notion of making notes in the margins of a book, whether it's a textbook, one of Shakespeare's plays or a modern classic. Kindle offers exactly this functionality, with the added bonus of making notes searchable, allowing you to easily find a note without having to thumb your way through hundreds of pages.

By default your notes are also backed up and synced between devices automatically, so if you change your Kindle at a later date, all your notes will be there waiting for you the next time you access a particular book.

Notes are added using the Kindle's keyboard, so if you think you're going to be a regular note-taker you may want to invest in a Kindle with a physical keyboard rather than the new smaller version without.

That said, it's perfectly possible to enter a reasonable amount of text using the virtual on-screen keyboard if you're in a bind or have already got a smaller device. We take you through the process in this in-depth guide.

"Notes are backed up and synced between devices automatically"

01: Move cursor into position

Before you can add a note you'll need to position your cursor at the location where you'd like the note to be attached to. Use the five-way controller to position your cursor before a word on the page (press up or down on your device to introduce the cursor to the specific page).

02: Start typing

Once your cursor is in position, just start typing to create a note at that location. If you've got a Kindle with a keyboard you can just start typing, but if you're using a 4th Generation Kindle you'll need to press the Keyboard button to bring up the on-screen keyboard before you can start typing away.

Creating, reading and deleting notes

Notes are a great way to add your own comments to a book on Kindle

Add a note
Adding a note is as simple as moving your cursor into position using the five-way controller, then starting to type! If you're using a 4th generation Kindle you can move your cursor into position and then press the keyboard button to bring up the on-screen keyboard for typing

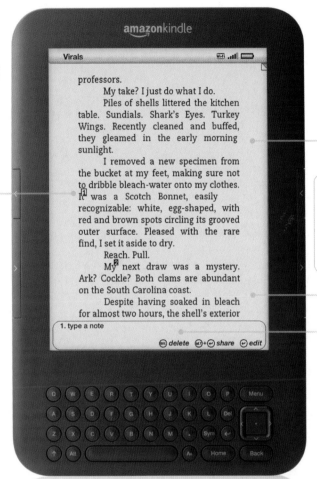

Viewing notes inline
Notes can be read inline by moving your cursor over the note. Use the five-way controller to move either up or down, then position it over the superscript note marker. A pop-up window will appear showing you the contents of the note

Notes on the page
Notes are shown on the page with a superscript number, indicating that there's a note hidden beneath the number. You can have as many notes as you like on a page, and they can also be accessed from the Notes & Marks screen

Deleting notes
You can delete a note directly from the inline view, or en masse by pressing the Menu button. From the pop-up menu, choose Notes & Marks, then locate the note you wish to delete and press the Delete button

03: Save your note
When you've finished typing, use the five-way controller to move your cursor so the Save Note button is highlighted. Click the centre button in the five-way controller to save the note. It will now appear as a superscript number next to the cursor.

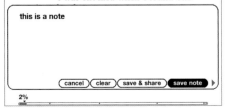

04: Delete a note
To delete a note, move your cursor into position so that it's over the note. You'll see the note appear in a little pop-up window either at the top or the bottom of the Kindle's screen. Press the Delete button to remove the note.

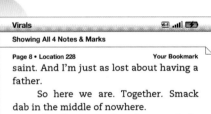

Use the dictionary

Find a word that you don't recognise? The Kindle comes complete with a built-in dictionary

It happens to all of us at some point; you're deeply engrossed in a book when all of a sudden you stumble across a word or phrase that you've never seen before. Having to put down a title and dig out a dictionary can really interrupt the flow of reading a book. The Kindle removes this distraction by providing a dictionary that's installed alongside the books on the device. This can be accessed at any time when reading a book.

When a problem word pops up, the Kindle can provide a full definition with just a few simple keystrokes. A registered Kindle device can access a number of dictionaries covering a variety of languages. It is also possible to download dictionaries that can provide translations from one language to another.

In the following tutorial we'll look at the basics of using the dictionary and have a quick glance at the extra functions available.

01: Find a definition

When reading a book use the five-way directional pad to move the cursor around the screen. When the cursor is in front of a recognised word in the dictionary, the Kindle will show a short definition at the top or bottom of the screen.

Kindle User's Guide

Kindle Store lets you see details about titles, read customer reviews and even download book samples. When you decide to make a |purchase, the Kindle Store uses the secure Amazon 1-Click payment method. To learn more about setting up your 1-Click payment method on your Manage Your Kindle page, go to www.kindle.com/support.

After you order, the Amazon Whispernet service delivers the item directly to your Kindle via

purchase v. [with obj.] 1 acquire (something) by paying for it; buy: Mr Gill spotted the manuscript at a local auction and purchased it for £1,500. ARCHAIC obtain or achieve ...

Press ⊙ for full definition, highlight, or note

02: Find out more

Press down on the five-way directional pad to bring up the context menu; 'full definition' will already be highlighted. Select this to bring up the full definition of the word. The page turn controls can be used to read more.

purchase
■ *v.* [with *obj.*]
1 acquire (something) by paying for it; buy: *Mr Gill spotted the manuscript at a local auction and purchased it for £1,500.*
    ‣ ARCHAIC obtain or achieve with effort or suffering: *the victory was purchased by the death of Rhiwallon.*
2 [NAUTICAL] haul up (a rope, cable, or anchor) by means of a pulley or lever.
■ *n.*
1 [*mass noun*] the action of buying something: *the large*

purchase | Q dictionary ▶

03: Even more definitions

While in the dictionary view, the word in the search box will stay highlighted. Clicking on this will open a new screen of similar words or phrases. This list can also be scanned through and looked up in the dictionary.

Oxford Dictionary of English

purchase
purchase tax
purchaser
purdah
pure
pure culture
pure line
pure mathematics
pure play
pure player
pure science
pure-bred

purchase | Q dictionary ▶

04: The context menu

The context menu also provides options to create a note or highlight a selection of text. These tools are useful when using the Kindle for reference purposes or simply for adding personalised touches or bookmarks to a title for future use.

Kindle User's Guide

cancel | create note | start highlight | full definition

Kindle Store lets you see details about titles, read customer reviews and even download book samples. When you decide to make a purchase, the Kindle Store uses the secure Amazon 1-Click payment method. To learn more about setting up your 1-Click payment method on your Manage Your Kindle page, go to www.kindle.com/support.

|After you order, the Amazon Whispernet service delivers the item directly to your Kindle via your Wi-Fi connection. Books are

29%

Switch between dictionaries

Your Kindle can store more than one dictionary and it's easy to change between them

The Amazon Kindle features a built-in dictionary, which we look at on the opposite page. However, this feature is not limited to a single language. Once a Kindle device is registered, you will have access to a selection of free dictionaries. These can be downloaded to the device at any time you like.

The available default choices of dictionaries cover US English, UK English, French, German, Brazilian Portuguese, Italian and Spanish languages. Depending on what language book is being read, it's possible to switch between dictionaries as and when the need arises. It's also possible to download and install

dictionaries that can translate words between languages. In most cases these titles can be purchased from the Amazon store.

In the following tutorial we'll look at downloading one of the free dictionaries and changing the currently selected default dictionary on a Kindle device.

01: Download a dictionary

Before we can change dictionaries, we need to download the new choice of dictionary to the Kindle device. From the device Home screen, press Menu and use the five-way directional pad to select View Archived Items from the menu screen.

02: Dictionary List options

The Archived Items list also displays the list of available dictionaries. Use the directional pad to highlight a dictionary and select it. The dictionary will start to automatically download to the Home screen. Once it has downloaded it will open up.

03: Changing the dictionary

To use the new dictionary when reading, press the Home button and then Menu. Select Settings and use the Previous/ Next page buttons until you see the Dictionaries section. Highlight the 'edit' link next to Dictionaries and select.

04: Select the dictionary

The next screen will display the currently used dictionary. Highlight the option marked Change Default and select it. On the next screen a list of dictionaries will appear. Using the directional pad, locate the recently downloaded dictionary and select it.

Listen to an audiobook

You may not have realised it, but a Kindle Keyboard is just as good at playing audiobooks as it is at displaying text!

The Kindle is first and foremost a reading device, and a very fine one at that. But like many portable electronic devices, it is also a relatively powerful computer and this means that it is capable of more than first meets the eye.

One of the most interesting non-book-related things that you can do with a Kindle is play back music or audiobook files. Audiobooks are simply audio versions of books, typically read by the author or someone with a nice speaking voice, and either read in full or in an abridged format.

You can get audiobooks by first downloading them from an online store, perhaps Amazon's own store, and then connecting your Kindle to your Mac or PC using the USB cable that you use to charge

the battery with. Once it mounts on the desktop, you can drag and drop your audio files into the folder called Music inside the Kindle drive that appears.

There's plenty of storage available so you will be able to drop a few different audiobooks onto the device. Sometimes they are split into different chapters and sometimes they are simply one large file containing the whole thing.

Disconnect from your computer and go into the Experimental section of the Menu. From here you will see the key commands for playing back the audiobooks. You can listen either using headphones via the on-board headphone jack, or using the built-in speaker. Simply press the 'F' key to skip to the next track.

"You can listen with headphones or using the built-in speaker"

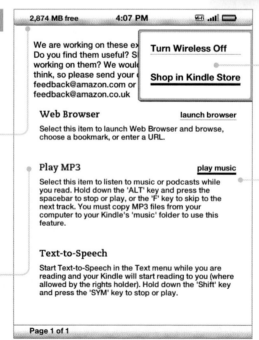

The Experimental section
Exploring audio playback on Kindle devices

Free space
Audiobooks use up much more space than eBooks, so you won't fit quite as many on at once. Use this free space readout to see how much space you have left

Instructions
In the Experimental section, these instructions tell you how to manage playback of audio files on your Kindle. It involves some simple key commands

Kindle Store
Audiobooks can be bought from a variety of places, including from Amazon. They can be dragged and dropped onto your Kindle or transferred directly from the store if you are connected over USB

Playback indicator
This section will change to read 'pause music' when audio is playing back. When it says 'play music' you know that nothing is currently playing back

01: Connect to your computer

Either download your audiobook files from an appropriate website like Amazon or Audible, or rip them to your hard drive from CD. Increasingly they are available online rather than on CD; they'll probably be in the MP3 format.

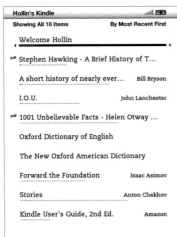

02: Connect the Kindle

Now connect the Kindle to your Mac or PC using the USB cable. When it appears on your desktop or in My Computer, open it. Now drag and drop the audio files into the folder called Music on the Kindle. Don't worry, your books will remain unchanged on the Home screen.

03: Go to the menu

Unplug your Kindle from the computer and it will return to the main Home screen. Click on the Menu button to be taken to the drop-down menu that lets you navigate the device. From this menu, use the five-way controller to navigate to the option labelled Experimental.

04: Go to the MP3 player

Press Enter to go into the Experimental section and then use the five-way controller to navigate down to the Play MP3 section. You can tell what option is selected because it will be underlined with a thick black line. This option says 'play music', but it can be used to play any audio files.

05: Play a file

Hold down the Alt key on the Kindle's keyboard and press the spacebar. The first track in the Music folder should start playing. You can press the spacebar a second time to stop playback. You can press the 'F' key to skip to the next track and tracks will play in name order.

06: Change the volume

The audiobook files will continue to play unless you stop them, or unless you open a book and activate the Text-to-Speech function. You can use the volume controls on the side of the Kindle to change the playback volume as you wish. This is how you play audiobooks on your Kindle.

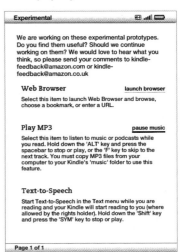

Using your Kindle

Subscribe to a newspaper

Use your Kindle to subscribe to magazines, newspapers and blogs – it's easy to set up and manage

One of the Kindle's lesser-known talents is that it can let you subscribe to various newspapers, magazines and even blogs, and wirelessly update them with new content directly to your device. This can all be set up directly from your Kindle and charged via your Amazon account, so there's no need to connect anything to a computer to make it happen. A lot of subscriptions will automatically renew so you have to keep an eye on them. On the other hand, a lot do come with a free trial period, so you are able to try them out with no risk to see if you like them.

The wireless updating is a particularly handy feature because it means you

don't have to manually update new content; it's delivered without you having to do anything at all. And in the case of newspapers or magazines, it means your daily or weekly copy is there ready when you set off on your morning commute.

Subscriptions are managed through the Kindle Store and this can be accessed directly from your device. Go to the Menu, click on Shop in Kindle Store and then in the Browse section choose the content type from Books, Newspapers, Magazines or Blogs. Navigate through to choose one that interests you and you will see the option to subscribe to it. Subscribe to as many as you like and they will all appear on your device.

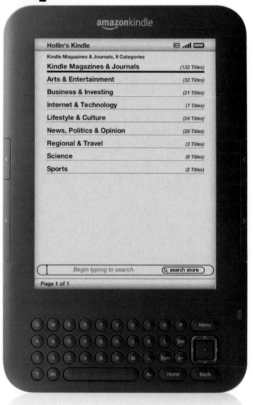

"You can subscribe to various newspapers, magazines and even blogs, and wirelessly update them"

Subscribing to content

How to work with subscriptions on your Kindle

Content type
You can choose to view Books, Newspapers, Magazines and also Blogs. Of these, the latter three can be subscribed to. Choose the ones you want

Search
You can run a search within the Store for specific keywords, which makes it much quicker to find a particular paper, blog or magazine without having to guess where it might be

Blogs
Blogs are a little different in that they aren't conventional media types like books, newspapers or magazines, but they are updated frequently and only quality, trusted blogs are listed in the Store

Recommended titles
Amazon wants to help you to find great new content and as such it will show you recommendations based on your previous Amazon buying habits and searches

01: Select the Store

From the Home screen press the Menu button and from the resulting pop-up window, choose Shop in Kindle Store. This will open the digital store. It will work more quickly if you are on a Wi-Fi network, but will also work over a 3G connection.

02: Press Enter

Hit the Enter key in the centre of the five-way controller to enter the Kindle Store. Under the Browse section at the top you will see the option to view Books, Magazines, Newspapers or Blogs. The latter three can be subscribed to. Click on Newspapers.

03: Choose a paper

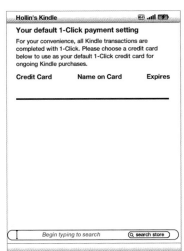

In the next step you can choose a paper. The first screen asks you to select by region and in this case we are going to choose Europe. Click through and then in the next screen, choose a paper from the list. You can view multiple pages if you want to see more.

04: Select a type

When you are taken through to the newspaper's subscription page you will see the details of the subscription options, including the monthly price and the current issue price. You can choose to buy a subscription or simply to buy the current issue.

05: Subscribe

Click over to the Subscribe button so that it is highlighted, then press Enter. You will be taken through to a screen that confirms your payment details as registered with Amazon. These will be the same ones you use for buying everything on Amazon so you should check they are up to date.

06: Confirm

When you confirm the payment, the details will be shown to you and you should immediately get a confirmation email from Amazon. When you return to your Home screen, you should see that now there's a new item containing the content you just subscribed to and this will be updated automatically with new content.

Remove Kindle content

You can store hundreds of documents on your Kindle, but once you've read a book you may want to get rid of it

As digital devices have become more popular, they have started to take over from conventional types of media. Certainly in the case of books, the Kindle has proved immensely successful for certain people in replacing hardbacks and paperbacks. Of course, real books will continue to exist, but it's nice to have the choice.

Just like with digital music stores, one of the best things about maintaining a digital book collection is that you have instant access to a vast potential library of content. No more going into high-street stores to be told there's a two-week wait for some obscure book that you want; the chances are that it's available online and can be downloaded instantly.

The wealth of stuff on offer can be a little daunting and you can use Collections to manage your content. But sometimes you just need to clear stuff off your Kindle.

It's not even that it uses up a lot of space on the device – it doesn't. But the more stuff you have on there, the more there is to wade through, and so if you've finished a book, you might want to delete it. Luckily this is straightforward to do from the device itself.

Your purchases are backed up automatically to your Amazon account, so you can choose to delete them permanently if you wish, or just from your Kindle device. Personal documents that you have stored on the Kindle can be deleted manually as well.

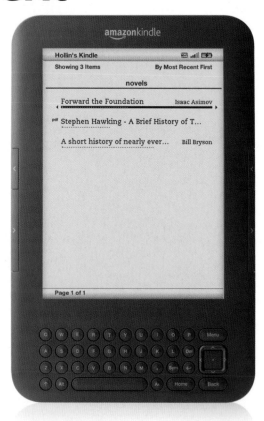

"The more stuff you have on there, the more there is to wade through"

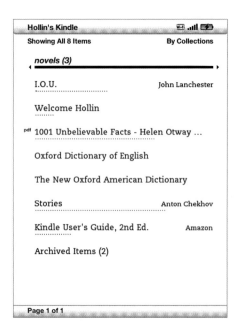

01: Go to your Home screen

Press the Home button to go back to the main Home screen. This is where you perform your file management and many other important tasks. Select a title from the list.

02: Remove the item

With a title selected, use the five-way controller and press the left arrow on that controller. This will give you a quick shortcut to delete the item. If you then press the Enter key in the centre of the controller, the title will be deleted from the device.

Remove content

Get rid of items from your Kindle

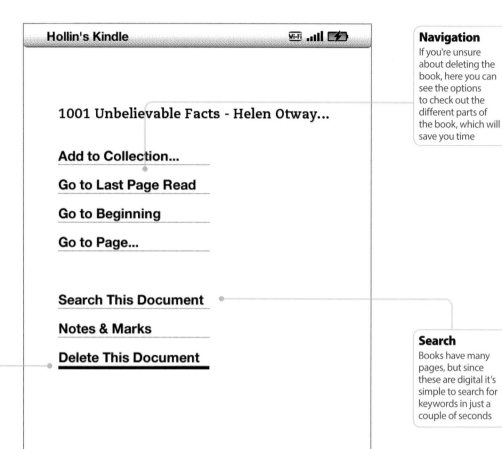

Hollin's Kindle

1001 Unbelievable Facts - Helen Otway...

Add to Collection...

Go to Last Page Read

Go to Beginning

Go to Page...

Search This Document

Notes & Marks

Delete This Document

Navigation
If you're unsure about deleting the book, here you can see the options to check out the different parts of the book, which will save you time

Delete
Permanently remove this item from your Kindle, either to free up space or simply because you have finished reading it

Search
Books have many pages, but since these are digital it's simple to search for keywords in just a couple of seconds

Hollin's Kindle

Stories
Anton Chekhov

Add to Collection...

Go to Last Page Read

Go to Beginning

Go to Location...

Book Description

Search This Book

Notes & Marks

Remove from Device

Stories
Anton Chekhov

03: Click right

Alternatively, click the right arrow on the five-way controller while the title is selected. This takes you to the contextual menu for that book. Navigate down to Remove from Device.

04: Remove the content

With the Remove option selected, click the Enter key and it will be immediately removed from the device. Repeat for as many titles as you want to remove. If they are backed up to your computer, they will be unaffected.

Hollin's Kindle

Showing All 7 Items   By Collections

novels (3)

I.O.U.   John Lanchester

Welcome Hollin

pdf 1001 Unbelievable Facts - Helen Otway ...

Oxford Dictionary of English

The New Oxford American Dictionary

Kindle User's Guide, 2nd Ed.   Amazon

Archived Items (2)

Page 1 of 1

Sort the order of your Home screen content

Managing lots of content can be tricky, so it helps to know how to sort it to make things easier

Ever since portable electronic devices went from needing you to stick content like games cartridges or CDs into them, the amount of content you can store on them has greatly increased. The Kindle only has a few gigabytes of storage on board, but this is still plenty of space when the average book only takes up a megabyte or two. Remember that there are a thousand megabytes in a gigabyte, so it's easy to store hundreds of books on a single Kindle if you want to. Of course this brings its own related issues, especially when it comes to finding your way around and sorting through the stuff that's on there.

Luckily, like many digital devices, the Kindle is able to help you with this. By going to the top of the main Home screen and choosing how to sort the content, you can choose to display it either by the most recently added titles first, by title or author alphabetically, or using Collections if you have them set up.

If you have a lot of stuff on there, but have read the older books and wanted to see the newer ones displayed first, you could sort the list by Most Recent First. Or, for a more logical sort order, choose to sort by Title or Author, and you should be able to easily find the books you want. Sorting the content on your Home screen is quick and easy.

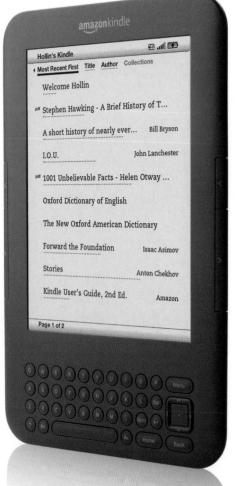

"For a more logical sort order, choose to sort by Title or Author"

01: Go to the Home screen
Go to the Home screen on your Kindle. If you are in another screen, press the Home button until you arrive back at the main screen. It should show a list of your titles.

02: Choose a sort type
Use the five-way cursor to navigate to the top of the screen so that the thick black line is under the Showing section. Then press the right arrow on the five-way controller to see the sorting options.

Sorting your Home screen

Understanding all the options you have

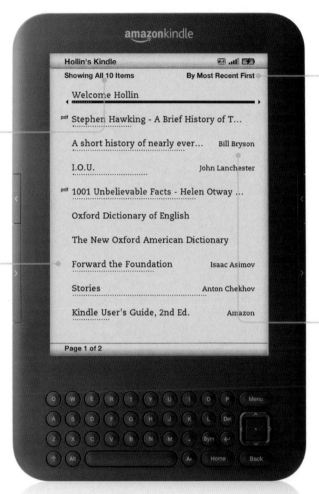

Sort type
This shows you how you are currently sorting your displayed list. Most Recent First will display the items that were most recently loaded at the top of the list

How many items
Here you see how many items you currently have loaded onto your device. If it's just a few, sorting is less important but if it's a lot it becomes vital

By Title
If you sort by Title, your Kindle will order the list alphabetically using the books' titles. This is one of the most common methods of sorting

Author
If you sort your list by author, the Kindle will sort the list alphabetically using the authors' surnames. Some people prefer this

RENAME YOUR FILES
eBooks do contain some metadata, which lets Kindle search and catalogue them more effectively. But you can manually rename your files on your Mac or PC to take more control over the way they are displayed. You're not limited to having them named the same way they are when you buy or download them.

03: Sort by Title
Use the five-way controller to select the Title option. You can see this is selected because it is underlined in black. Press the Enter button. This will sort your list by book title. Go back to the list to see this in action.

04: Sort by Author
If you prefer you can sort the list by the name of the book's author. Select Author and hit the Enter button in the middle of the five-way controller. The list will then be sorted based on author names. You can change the sort settings at any time.

Create a Collection

Manage your Kindle content more effectively by creating your very own Collections on the Home screen

When you start to accumulate more and more content on your Kindle, it can become fiddly to navigate and manage it all. Remember that it doesn't just do eBooks, it can also store digital editions of newspapers, PDF files, audiobooks and personal documents that you load onto it. There's quite a lot that you can put on one, so it makes sense to start to organise things more effectively if you get to this point.

To help you with this, the Kindle supports Collections and, as you might imagine, these are simply a way of grouping content into more easily manageable sections that you name and control yourself. From the main menu you can choose to create a Collection and then

assign it a name using either the manual keyboard or the on-screen keyboard, depending on which device you have. Individual items can then be assigned to Collections and your Home screen list sorted by Collection. Collections are also stored wirelessly on Amazon's website so you can sync them across your Kindle devices, and content can appear in more than one Collection.

It's a great way to set up a Collection of novels, a Collection of audiobooks and a Collection of textbooks on your device, so that they are easier to access. When you delete a Collection, the content stored in it is not deleted – only the Collection is removed. Think of it like throwing away a folder, but saving its contents.

"Content can appear in more than one Collection"

Working with Kindle Collections
Get the most out of your Kindle by organising content

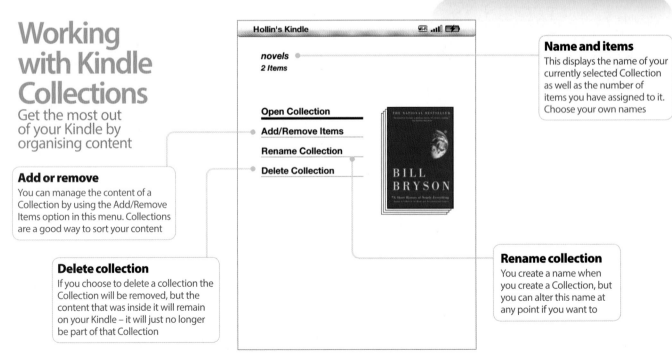

Add or remove
You can manage the content of a Collection by using the Add/Remove Items option in this menu. Collections are a good way to sort your content

Delete collection
If you choose to delete a collection the Collection will be removed, but the content that was inside it will remain on your Kindle – it will just no longer be part of that Collection

Name and items
This displays the name of your currently selected Collection as well as the number of items you have assigned to it. Choose your own names

Rename collection
You create a name when you create a Collection, but you can alter this name at any point if you want to

01: Create a Collection

From the Home screen, click the Menu button and you are taken to the main menu. Use the five-way controller to click down to the option called Create New Collection which should be underlined in thick black to show you it is selected. Press the Enter button in the centre of the five-way controller.

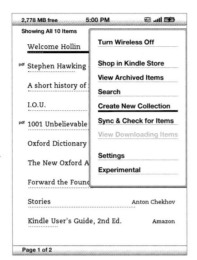

02: Assign a name

From the resulting window, use the keyboard to enter a name for the Collection. Then navigate to the 'save' button in this screen and press Enter. In the next screen, select an item from the list and then press the right arrow on the five-way controller.

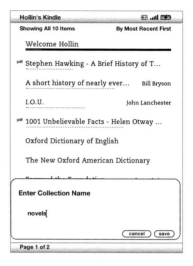

03: Add to Collection

From this menu, select Add To Collection. This will show you a list of Collections and you can choose which one to add your book to. You will see the option 'Add to this collection' available so choose a collection and then press Enter to assign the item to that collection.

04: Add another

Select another item from your Home Screen and repeat the process. Note that if you click Enter a second time from this screen it will have the effect of removing that item from the collection. Go back to the Home screen and your collection should be visible.

05: Rename the Collection

Select your collection in the Home screen – it should be underlined in thick black – and press the right arrow on the five-way controller. Here you will see various options including the option to rename the collection, if you have changed your mind. Press Enter to rename it.

06: Delete a Collection

From the same screen you can also delete a collection using the 'delete' option. From the Home screen you can delete a collection by selecting it and pressing the left arrow on the five-way controller. This gives you a quick delete option.

Add or remove Collection items

Collections are a great way to manage your content, and they're easy to use as well

Collections are a clever way to organise content on your Kindle and keep everything in good order. Imagine you have quite a few novels and newspapers, but you want to organise them into categories, Collections would be an easy way to achieve that, and they're designed to be simple to add content to as well as remove content from, all without having to sync anything to your Mac or PC.

It's all done on the device. In fact Collections are shared wirelessly, so if you do create or modify one, that data is stored online in your Amazon account, and will be updated on any other Kindles registered to the same account. In reality it's really simple to manage groups of books and other content even if you

have several devices. You can mix and match content within a Collection, they don't all have to be books, or newspapers or audiobooks.

And if you choose to delete a Collection, the content that was grouped inside that Collection isn't deleted, it's just 'unbundled' and remains available. Only the Collection is affected, not the data stored inside it.

You might decide that once you have read a book, for example, you no longer want it to be in your Unread collection, and it would be easy in a case like this to simply remove it. Or, add a new book to the same Collection.

Use Collections to more sensibly manage the content on your Kindle. We show you how to do it here.

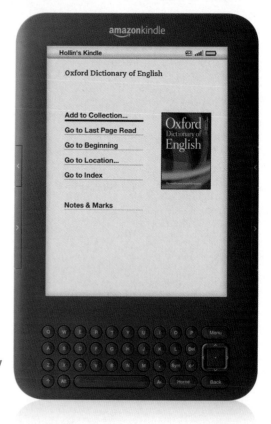

"Use Collections to more sensibly manage the content on your Kindle"

01: Go to a Collection

Create a Collection and then go to your content list, which you can see by pressing the Home button to go to your Home screen. Select an item in this list – say a novel – and then press the right arrow on the five-way controller.

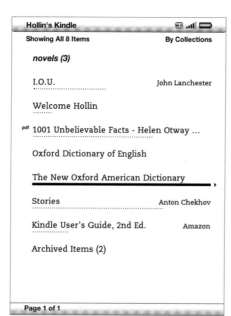

02: Add to Collection

From the resulting screen, you can choose to add this item to a Collection. If you click Add To Collection, you will see a list of the available collections. Select a Collection and then click the Enter button to add the book to it.

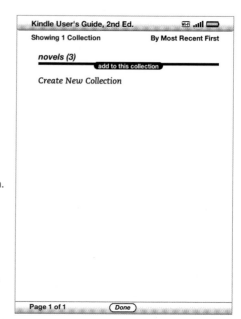

Adding to a Collection

Add or remove stuff from your Collections

Add to Collection
Select an item like a novel and then choose to add it to a Collection. You can have multiple Collections and they are nondestructive, so your books are unaffected if you delete them

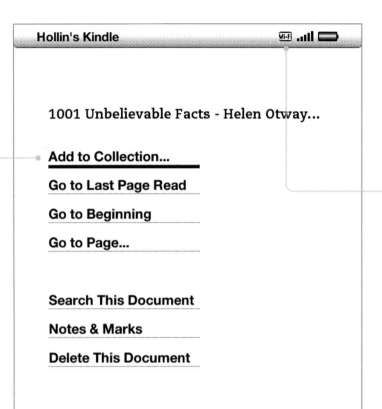

Hollin's Kindle Wi-Fi

1001 Unbelievable Facts - Helen Otway...

Add to Collection...

Go to Last Page Read

Go to Beginning

Go to Page...

Search This Document

Notes & Marks

Delete This Document

Wi-Fi
Your Kindle will have Wi-Fi and maybe also 3G. These enable it to wirelessly download data as well as communicate with Amazon's servers, updating your Collections as you add to or remove from them

UP TO YOU
An item on your Kindle, like a book, can be shared in as many Collections as you like. So a book may be part of Novels, but also Crime. It's up to you how much or how little of this you do, but it's good habit to get into.

03: View Collection
Now, go back to your Home screen and navigate to the Collection. Click Enter to view it and you will see all the items that you have assigned to it, in this case, three books. Select one of the books.

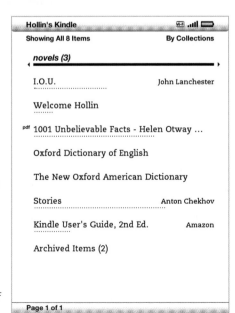

Hollin's Kindle Wi-Fi

Showing All 8 Items — By Collections

novels (3)

I.O.U. — John Lanchester

Welcome Hollin

pdf 1001 Unbelievable Facts - Helen Otway ...

Oxford Dictionary of English

The New Oxford American Dictionary

Stories — Anton Chekhov

Kindle User's Guide, 2nd Ed. — Amazon

Archived Items (2)

Page 1 of 1

04: Remove an item
With an item in a Collection selected, click the left arrow on the five-way controller and you will see an option appear to remove the book from the Collection. If you select this and press Enter, the book will be de-assigned from the Collection.

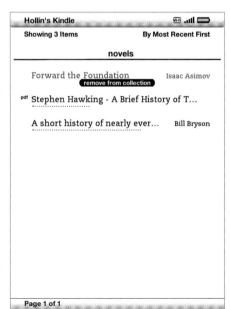

Hollin's Kindle Wi-Fi

Showing 3 Items — By Most Recent First

novels

Forward the Foundation — Isaac Asimov
remove from collection

pdf Stephen Hawking - A Brief History of T...

A short history of nearly ever... — Bill Bryson

Page 1 of 1

Import your Collections

If you upgrade, it's possible to import your book Collections from one unit to another

The Kindle has already gone through a number of iterations and will continue to do so. The problem is, once you've had a device for a while it becomes your own personalised portable library. Should the time come to upgrade a Kindle or replace a faulty device, the idea of having to start organising your titles again from scratch is far from appealing. Thankfully the Kindle includes a feature that can import Collections from another device. Collections are your own personal groups of books that can be based around any topic, be it a genre, author or any other theme that takes your fancy.

This process only organises content that is already on a device; it won't download any titles that are not yet on the device itself. Before importing Collections, it is necessary to open the Archived Items folder and download any items that you wish to have automatically organised into a collection.

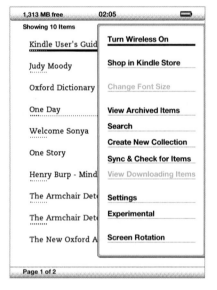

01: Turn Wireless on

The first step is to activate the data connection on your Kindle device. For a Wi-Fi connection, press the Menu button from the Home screen. The option to activate the Wi-Fi can be found at the top of the menu.

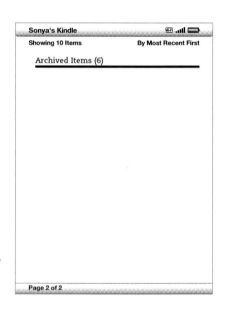

02: View Archived Items

The first step is to view the Archived Items list. This page is usually stored on the final page of your downloaded items. Scrolling through to the final page will show the link to the list of archived items.

03: Archive list shortcut

Should your Kindle feature a large selection of book titles, a shortcut to the Archived Items list is also available from the menu on the home page. Press the Menu key and select 'View Archived Items' to access the list.

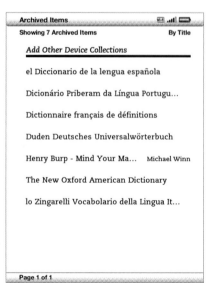

04: Add Other Collections

Once you're in the list of archived items the option to Add Other Device Collections can be located at the top of the screen. Select this and from the next screen select the collection that you would like to import.

Downloading archived items

Even if you have deleted content, you can re-download titles from your archive

The Archived Items section is a crucial part of the Kindle experience. Over time, the amount of books that you will download will significantly increase. Either due to space constraints or the need to keep things organised, it may become necessary to remove certain titles from the device from time to time. The Archived Items menu is the part of the device that syncs with Amazon to keep track of every purchased title. When an item is deleted it still remains as an entry on this list. Should the need arise to download a deleted title again it can be located within the Archived Items list and selected. This function is particularly useful when a user upgrades their Kindle device. Once a new device is logged in to an existing Amazon account the Archived Items list will appear. This list will feature every previously downloaded title that the user can easily download to their new device via a data connection.

01: Activate Wireless
Downloading items requires an active data connection, so make sure that Wi-Fi is turned on. 3G Kindle devices will connect automatically.

02: Archived Items
You need to navigate to the Archived Items list, which you can do directly from the main Menu as shown here. We run through the full steps in the tutorial on the previous page.

03: Locate a title
The Archived Items list displays every title that has been downloaded using that particular Amazon account. Using the five-way directional pad, highlight a title and click it to start downloading.

04: Download a book
The download screen will now appear. If the user stays on this screen the book will open automatically once it's downloaded. Alternatively, pressing the Home button will leave the download in the background so the Kindle can still be used.

View and change the time

Getting lost in a good book is always fun, but sometimes you need to keep track of the time while you're reading!

The Kindle has many advantages over a paperback book, such as audio playback, wireless newspaper subscriptions and the ability to store hundreds of books on a device that fits in your pocket. But as well as these headline-grabbing features it has more basic tools that are still really useful to have at your fingertips. It might seem simple, but it's really useful to be able to have a digital clock with you when you're sitting and reading. Getting lost in a book is great and it's part of the reason people love their Kindles, but it's not so helpful if you miss your plane because you were so absorbed in reading!

Luckily the Kindle does have a clock and you can set this manually if you like. Again this isn't as crazy as it sounds: imagine you are on holiday in a country in a different time zone from your own. It's really useful to be able to go in and set the time yourself. After all a clock is no good if it's an hour or two out.

The Kindle's battery life is also excellent so you won't need to worry about the clock running it down. In fact it's hidden for most of the time, unless you press the Menu button to reveal it, so it doesn't use up too much power. If you're reading and need to quickly know the time, just tap the Menu button.

"If you're reading and need to quickly know the time, just tap the Menu button"

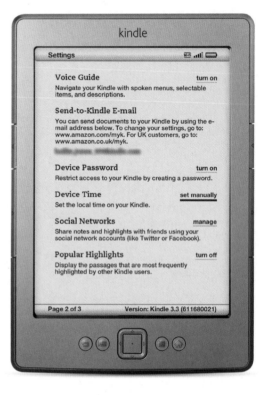

01: Check the time

While you are reading a book, click the Menu button on your Kindle and the menu will appear without taking you away from the book – it remains in the background. At the same time, the time will appear in the menu bar at the top.

02: Change the time

If you're in a different time zone you might want to change your Kindle's clock to reflect this and keep you up to speed. Start by going back to the Home screen by pressing the Home button.

Setting the time

Keep your clock correct with the right time settings

Menu bar
When you press the Menu button, Kindle will display the time here. This is a handy shortcut to know about and won't take you away from your books

Time setting
Use the arrows on the five-way controller to manually set the time in hours and minutes. Hold the controller down to cycle through the numbers more quickly

AUTO TIME
Kindle models that support 3G data connections are able to set their time automatically. They do this by connecting to time servers over the air and auto updating themselves, even if you are in another country. This can help keep you up to date.

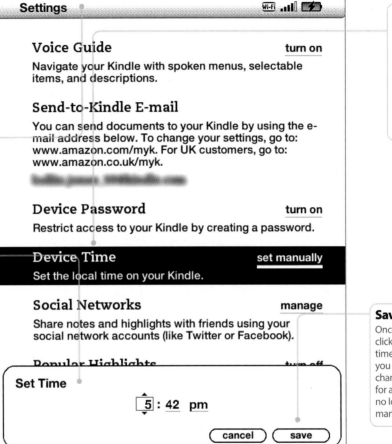

Settings

Voice Guide   turn on
Navigate your Kindle with spoken menus, selectable items, and descriptions.

Send-to-Kindle E-mail
You can send documents to your Kindle by using the e-mail address below. To change your settings, go to: www.amazon.com/myk. For UK customers, go to: www.amazon.co.uk/myk.

Device Password   turn on
Restrict access to your Kindle by creating a password.

Device Time   set manually
Set the local time on your Kindle.

Social Networks   manage
Share notes and highlights with friends using your social network accounts (like Twitter or Facebook).

Popular Highlights   turn off

Set Time

5 : 42 pm

cancel   save

Page 2 of 3   Version: Kindle 3.3 (611680021)

Device Time
Inside the Settings menu, you can set the Kindle's clock. This is useful to be able to do, especially if you are going on holiday to a country that's in a different time zone

Save
Once you are done, click to 'save' the time, or hit 'cancel' if you decide you have changed your mind for any reason and no longer want to manually set the time

03: Press Menu

Press the Menu button and, in the menu, navigate to the Settings section. Then use the Next Page button on the right-hand edge of the device to navigate to the second page of options. Now Scroll down to the Device Time option.

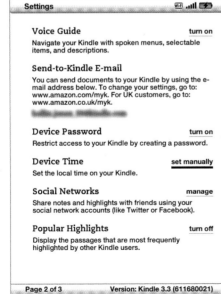

04: Set the time

Press Enter and use the up and down arrows on the five-way controller to manually set the time. When you're done, scroll over to 'save' and click Enter. The Kindle's time is now set as you instructed.

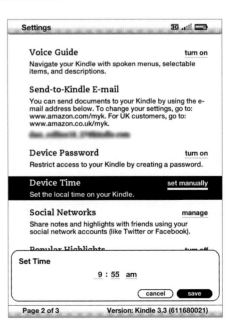

The next step

In-depth guides to get more from your Kindle

Key pick
Page 128
Use a Kindle Keyboard
to play Minesweeper
and GoMoku!

Enter Password

Press ⊖ to submit
Move the 5-way down if you forgot your password.

Emily
Dickinson

Slide and release the power switch to wake

Page 110
■ *Lock up your Kindle with a password*

The Times and The Sunday Times

THE ❧ TIMES
Kindle Edition, © 2012 Times Newspapers Limited.
Queen defends beleaguered Church

Credit: Matt Dunhamm/AFP/Getty Images
Dr Rowan Williams displays the ampulla and coronation
spoon, used at the Queen's coronation in 1953, during
yesterday's reception at Lambeth Palace
Ruth Gledhill | Religion Correspondent | 700 words
The Queen delivered her strongest defence of the

next article: The new atheists have succeeded only in uniting ...
View Sections & Articles   next article ▶

Page 112
■ *Keep hold of your favourite articles from periodicals*

The M...

"Better...
enginee...
"We...
too, that t...
of the cour...
"We shal...
we have first...
replied the engine...
"But to-morrow, c... shall
you be in a state to bear the fatigue of the ascent?"
♪"I hope so," replied the engineer, "provided you
and Pencroft, my boy, show yourselves quick and
clever hunters."
"Captain," said the sailor, "since you are speaking
of game, if on my return, I was as certain of roasting it
as I am of bringing it back--"
"Bring it back all the same, Pencroft," replied
Harding.
It was then agreed that the engineer and the

Enter Your Message
A link to your highlight will be appended to your message.

an interesting turn of phrase

71 characters left   cancel   share

12%

Page 120
■ *Get involved by sharing on social networking sites*

Page 144
■ *Get online and convert to Kindle's mobi format*

Page 154
■ *Pick up where you left off on a home computer*

Key pick
Page 122
How to redeem an
Amazon gift certificate for
lots of Kindle eBooks

118
■ *Public Notes enable you to
share your thoughts with the
Kindle community*

Update your Kindle's software

Keeping your Kindle's system software up to date means you can take full advantage of the latest features

One of the best things about modern electronic devices like the Kindle is that they rarely retain the same set level of functionality that they have when you buy them. Manufacturers are always adding new features and fixing problems, and these things are brought to your device through software updates.

The Kindle's operating system is what makes it run and it's stored on the on-board memory. By applying software updates you can make sure your Kindle has access to the latest features and tools, and these are almost always made available for free. Updating isn't a complicated process, though it's one that you have to carry out manually – there's no facility to have the device automatically update

itself. It essentially involves downloading a file from the relevant section of Amazon's website to your computer, then dragging and dropping this file to the Kindle while it's connected via a USB cable. When the file has transferred you can then go into the relevant section on the Kindle and tell it to perform the update. It's important not to unplug it or try to use it while this is happening to ensure the update completes successfully.

In a recent update, Amazon added the ability to download your own archived personal documents and also added Whispersync to enable the synchronising of these documents across all your Kindle devices. Follow our simple guide to make sure your Kindle is up to date.

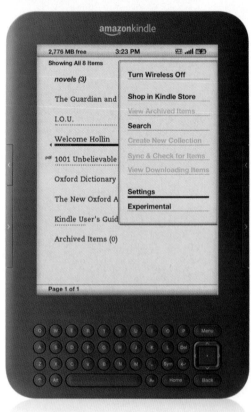

"You can make sure your Kindle has access to the latest features"

01: Check your version

To see what version of the system you already have installed, press the Menu button and then go to the Settings option. Look at the bottom-right corner of the screen and you will see Version: Kindle and then a number.

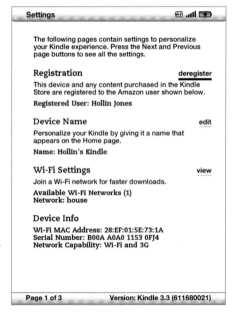

02: Get the update

Go to Amazon's website and download the latest version of the system, if this is newer than the one you have. Connect your Kindle via USB and when it appears on your desktop, drag the file to the Kindle drive icon.

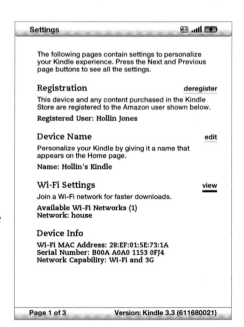

Updating your system

Find out your Kindle's operating system number

Wi-Fi
It will help if you have a Kindle Keyboard to be on a Wi-Fi network, as you will be able to get the update sent to your device by using Sync and Check for Items in the main menu

WIRELESS SYNC
Owners of the Kindle Keyboard and 3G models should be able to get the software update wirelessly. Press the Menu button and choose Sync and Check for Items. If an update is available you will be notified and you can perform the Update Your Kindle step as detailed below.

Settings Wi-Fi ..ull 🔋

The following pages contain settings to personalize your Kindle experience. Press the Next and Previous page buttons to see all the settings.

Registration   deregister
This device and any content purchased in the Kindle Store are registered to the Amazon user shown below.
Registered User: Hollin Jones

Device Name   edit
Personalize your Kindle by giving it a name that appears on the Home page.
Name: Hollin's Kindle

Wi-Fi Settings   view
Join a Wi-Fi network for faster downloads.
**Available Wi-Fi Networks (1)
Network: house**

Device Info
**Wi-Fi MAC Address: 28:EF:01:5E:73:1A
Serial Number: B00A A0A0 1153 0FJ4
Network Capability: Wi-Fi and 3G**

Page 1 of 3   Version: Kindle 3.3 (611680021)

Registration
You will have to register your Kindle with the same details you use to log into your Amazon account. This allows you to buy content, synchronise data and also helps with the updating process

Device info
Check your Kindle's network capability in this section of the Settings screen. It will have Wi-Fi and possibly also 3G

Version number
The all-important version number, which you can compare against the version number of the latest software as found on Amazon's help website to see if an update to your device is needed

---

03: Start software update
Now eject your Kindle from the computer and press the Menu key. The option called Update Your Kindle will be available if the software update is newer than the version already installed.

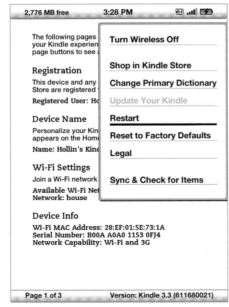

04: Verify the update
The update process will take a minute or two and your Kindle will restart itself several times. Once it has finished, return to the Settings screen and check at the bottom-right that the software is up to date.

Set a password

Make sure your Kindle stays safe by securing it with a password

Whether you're security-conscious or not, it pays to protect your Kindle device with a password. After all, what if you leave it somewhere, and a stranger picks it up and starts making purchases using your Amazon account? Or perhaps you store personal documents on your device that you don't want to fall into the wrong hands, in which case even if you fail to retrieve it, at least none of your sensitive data will be scrutinised by unauthorised eyes.

It is easy to apply a password to your device; simply press the 'Menu' button while on the home screen, go to 'Settings' and navigate to the second page of options to see the 'Device Password'. Enter a password twice to set it, and provide a hint so that in the event of forgetting your password, the hint will help you remember. Once you have set it up, you will need to enter your password every time you awake your device from sleeping.

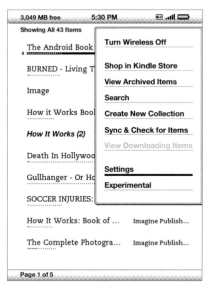

01: Go to Settings
To start the process of protecting your device with a password, press the 'Menu' button on the Kindle's home screen, and then use the five-way controller to navigate your way down to the 'Settings' section.

02: Go to Device Password
There are three Settings screens for your Kindle device, so use the 'Next Page' button (the larger of the two side buttons) to scroll to the second page, where you will see an option called 'Device Password'. Select it.

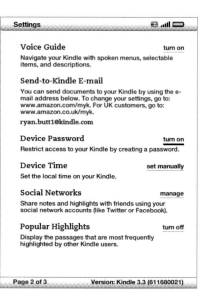

03: Enter password
You will now be prompted to enter a password, which you will have to do twice and then add a password hint. Enter your password directly from your Kindle Keyboard; press the 'Sym' key to enter numbers or press the Keyboard button on a standard Kindle.

04: Password protection
Now, whenever your device goes to sleep, you will be prompted to enter your password upon waking it up. If you forget it, then you can move the controller down to get a hint. Try to make it something that you'll remember!

Keep subscription content

Stop the Kindle automatically deleting the content you want to keep

Taking out subscriptions from the Kindle Store is easy, and all of them come with a free 14-day trial so that you can try each one before actually paying, which is a great way to determine if a magazine or newspaper is for you by sampling how well it is formatted for Kindle.

When you are subscribed to a particular periodical, older issues of newspapers and magazines appear inside a grouping called 'Periodicals: Back Issues'. Selecting this takes you to a screen that displays all of the back issues that you have on your device. However, your Kindle will automatically delete newspaper and magazine issues that are more than seven issues old in order to free up space on your device for new content. An exclamation mark next to a magazine or newspaper will indicate that it will be deleted soon – so what do you do if you would like to keep a copy of an issue? Here's what…

01: Take out a subscription

The good thing about Kindle newspapers and magazines is that they all come with a free 14-day trial, so you can sample the product before you buy it. Go to the Kindle Store and search the 'Newspapers' and 'Magazines' sections for items to subscribe to.

02: Getting issues

When you click on a particular item's info page, you will see the option to 'Subscribe now with 14-day Free Trial'. Select this and a message will appear to confirm your purchase and inform you that your item will be transferred to your home screen.

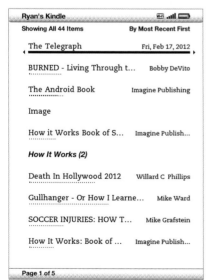

03: Open your item

Older issues of newspapers and magazines appear inside a grouping called 'Periodicals: Back Issues'. Selecting the grouping takes you to a screen that displays your back issues. To keep an older issue, open the specific issue from your home screen.

04: Keeping older issues

When the issue is displayed on your screen, press the 'Menu' button, then choose the 'Keep This Issue' option. Once done, you will then see the word 'Keep' to the left of the issue title on your home screen.

Make, view and edit clippings

Saving news articles from your favourite periodicals allows you to share their contents wherever and however you want

One of the great conveniences of using the Kindle compared to traditional newspapers and magazines is the capability to perform otherwise impossible tasks. How often, for example, have you wished you could somehow commit a particular column or news article to memory for later debate and dissection? Sometimes it's hard enough to remember which page or periodical the article was on a mere 20 minutes later, let alone the crux of the discussion within.

Wouldn't it be wonderful if you could quickly and conveniently save those words while you're reading, and then recall them quickly at a moment's notice? With the Kindle it really is that easy, and all it takes is a few button presses.

Doing so simply requires you to 'clip' your periodical to the My Clippings file. This is the file on your Kindle that stores all of your notes, highlights, bookmarks and clippings you've made over your entire Kindle book collection. Not only can you quickly and easily recall the content of this file for later consumption, but you can even port them over to your computer in the form of a standard text file allowing you to edit, print or even send it on to family, friends or work colleagues via email and more.

"It really is that easy, and all it takes is a few button presses"

01: Access your content

Whether you're using the keyboard-style Kindle or newer, keyless model, simply open the blog, newspaper or magazine you wish to save a clipping from by accessing them from your home screen (by clicking the Home button).

The Times and The Sunday Times

THE TIMES
Kindle Edition, © 2012 Times Newspapers Limited.
Queen defends beleaguered Church

Credit: Matt Dunhamm/AFP/Getty Images
Dr Rowan Williams displays the ampulla and coronation spoon, used at the Queen's coronation in 1953, during yesterday's reception at Lambeth Palace
Ruth Gledhill | Religion Correspondent | 700 words
The Queen delivered her strongest defence of the

next article: The new atheists have succeeded only in uniting ...
View Sections & Articles   next article ▶

02: Make a selection

One you have found a suitable article you'd like to save for future dissection, all you need to do is click the Menu button and, using the five-way directional controller, scroll down to the option marked 'Clip This Article' and select it.

The Times and The Sunday...   8:53 AM

THE TIMES
Kindle Edition, ©

MPs' visit to further stoke
Select committee t

| Turn Wireless Off |
| Shop in Kindle Store |
| Search This Issue |
| Clip This Article |
| Sync to Furthest Page Read |
| Add a Note or Highlight |
| View Notes & Marks |
| Keep This Issue |

Credit: Enrique Marcarian/Reuters
President Kirchner announced that Argentina would protest to the UN over Britain's 'militarisation' of the Falklands last week
Deborah Haynes | Defence Editor | 569 words

next article: Duke in Falklands rescue
View Sections & Articles   next article ▶

Inside your clippings

An in-depth look at your clippings document

Headlines

Each entry in your clippings document is given a new title. Using the Page Up and Down buttons it's easy to cycle through your entries

Create highlights

Once you've found the clipping you were interested in you can simply press the button in the five-way controller to create a highlight of a particularly noteworthy passage

MORE OPTIONS

Once you've found the clipping you wanted to reread, you can use the Menu button to open up further options from the menu. From here it's possible to search your document, add a bookmark or view the previously made notes and marks.

Snip snip

Each time you add a new clipping, bookmark or highlight, your clippings document is appended. These line breaks are the separators between each entry

Date and time

Since news clippings from the same periodical have similar names, the date and time of the clipping can be used to identify individual entries at a glance

---

Kindle device screen showing:

amazonkindle

Argentina has never given up its claim to the islands, which it calls the Malvinas. Britain rejects the claim and insists that the islands' 3,000 inhabitants have done so for nine generations and have a right to self-determination. The islanders see themselves as part of Britain.
==========
My Clippings
- Bookmark Loc. 272 | Added on Wednesday, February 15, 2012, 01:36 PM

==========
The Times and The Sunday Times (Times Newspapers Limited.)
- Clipping Loc. 3-37 | Added on Thursday, February 16, 2012, 08:26 AM

Queen defends beleaguered Church Credit: Matt Dunhamm/AFP/Getty Images Dr Rowan Williams displays the ampulla and coronation spoon, used at the Queen's coronation in 1953, during yesterday's reception at Lambeth Palace Ruth Gledhill | Religion Correspondent | 700 words The Queen delivered her strongest defence of the Church of England yesterday, describing its role in society as under-appreciated, after a week in which religion has come under intense attack. Speaking at Lambeth Palace, the London home

89%

03: View your clipping

When you wish to recall your clipped article, simply go to the home screen (by pressing the Home button) and select My Clippings. It should be near the top of your book collection. Turn the page down to the last entry – it will be your most recent clipping.

and all those lovely new backdrops in the game for all to enjoy, it's a great time to be hammering away at the print screen key. Probably the best time since Apocrypha, in fact. What we're after is much the same as what always ask for ; beautiful images at a high-ish resolution and the UI turned off, along with a few lines about what is going on and where (where is especially important). Don't forget to include your character name in your email either. Those that have their images published will earn themselves 100m ISK and if I'm organised they'll get a free magazine as well. Get snapping and sent your pics and text to postcards@mmmpublishing.com by downtime on Monday. Good luck and enjoy EVE beyond Incarna. Posted: Nov 29 11:15 am
==========
The Times and The Sunday Times (Times Newspapers Limited.)
- Clipping Loc. 3-33 | Added on Wednesday, February 15, 2012, 09:01 AM

MPs' visit to the Falkland Islands further stokes Argentina fury Select committee to inspect British defences Credit: Enrique Marcarian/Reuters President Kirchner announced that Argentina would protest to the UN over Britain's 'militarisation' of the Falklands last week Deborah Haynes | Defence Editor | 569 words MPs will visit the Falklands next month to inspect

89%

04: Edit your clipping

If you'd like to share or edit your clipping via computer you can simply connect your Kindle via USB, open its storage folder on your computer and look in the Documents folder – it will be listed alongside all your books.

Text editor window titled "My Clippings.txt" showing:

Government is pursuing its usual political nonsense," he added. The maj member committee are scheduled to fly next month to Mount Pleasant, the the Falklands and part of a sprawling British military base. It is the committee members have travelled to the islands since 1999. Argentina up its claim to the islands, which it calls the Malvinas. Britain reje insists that the islands' 3,000 inhabitants have done so for nine gene a right to self-determination. The islanders see themselves as part of
==========
My Clippings
- Bookmark Loc. 272 | Added on Wednesday, February 15, 2012, 01:36 PM

==========
The Times and The Sunday Times (Times Newspapers Limited.)
- Clipping Loc. 3-37 | Added on Thursday, February 16, 2012, 08:26 AM

Queen defends beleaguered Church Credit: Matt Dunhamm/AFP/Getty Images Williams displays the ampulla and coronation spoon, used at the Queen's 1953, during yesterday's reception at Lambeth Palace Ruth Gledhill | Re Correspondent | 700 words The Queen delivered her strongest defence of England yesterday, describing its role in society as under-appreciated, which religion has come under intense attack. Speaking at Lambeth Pala home of the Archbishop of Canterbury, in her first public engagement to Diamond Jubilee, she delivered a rare rebuke to critics of establishmen "We should remind ourselves of the significant position of the Church o nation's life. The concept of our established Church is occasionally mi I believe, commonly under-appreciated," she said. The Queen's intervent with growing tensions between secularism and religion. Last Friday the Society won a court victory when a judge ruled that prayers could not b of council meetings. The society then vowed to try to outlaw prayers in Tuesday, the Richard Dawkins Foundation, which propagates a vehement at published a survey claiming many people who identified themselves as Ch take a literal approach to Christian doctrine and the Bible. Baroness Muslim in the Cabinet, then defended religion during a trip to the Vat Pope. The Queen, dressed in cardinal red, began her address to the lead nine main faith traditions by paying tribute to "the particular mission and the general value of faith in this country". She added: "Its role Anglicanism to the exclusion of other religions. Instead, the Church ho protect the free practice of all faiths in this country." The Queen sai

The next step

Transfer My Clippings files

Whether you want to share or archive your My Clippings document, you can do so easily using any computer

Among other things, all of your Highlights (your favourite noteworthy passages from books, see page 84), Clippings (articles from newspapers and magazines) and notes (personal reminders added to one of your Kindle books) are stored on your Kindle in a file called My Clippings.

Your My Clippings content is accessible directly from the Home screen on your Kindle, but should you want to share the document's content with a friend via email or social networking site, or append passages to your work or school project, you can connect your Kindle to your PC and access the file

directly from there. The My Clippings document is a very basic PC-compatible document type that can be read and edited by almost any computer or operating system in the world. It can be opened by any Windows, Mac OS X or Linux PC without the need of any extra software. The document itself can be copied directly to your computer whole, or edited and resaved on your Kindle hard drive – the choice is yours.

Accessing your My Clippings document content is very simple, and works the same way regardless of whether you have a Keyboard Kindle or the newer, keyboardless model.

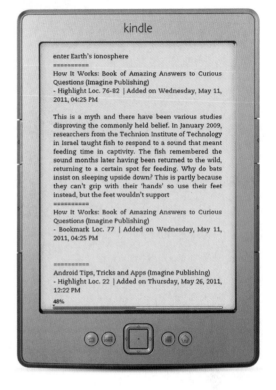

"The My Clippings document… can be read and edited by almost any computer or operating system"

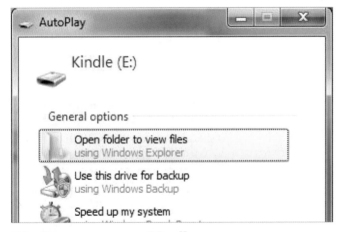

01: Connect your Kindle

Using the USB charging cable that came with your Kindle, connect the mini-USB end into your Kindle and the other end into a free USB port in your computer. An AutoPlay (or equivalent) window should appear asking if you'd like to open the files on the Kindle hard drive.

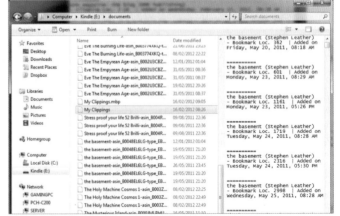

02: Access My Clippings.txt

If the AutoPlay box doesn't appear, just access My Computer to see your hard drives. Double-click on the entry called 'Kindle' to open the main Kindle folder which is made up of Documents, Audible and Music folders. Double-click on Documents.

Your Clippings document explained

How the My Clippings document is laid out

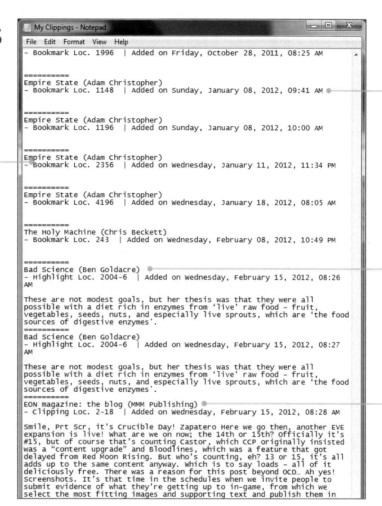

Bookmarks

All the bookmarks you've ever made are stored on your My Clippings.txt document. Don't forget that if you delete them from the file, they'll also be deleted from your Kindle

BETTER SAFE THAN SORRY

When accessing your Kindle-stored My Clippings document, instead of opening and editing it directly from your Kindle, we recommend copying the whole document to your computer and working with the copied version as opposed to the original. Doing this limits the possibility of accidentally deleting bookmarks or notes.

Date order

Everything in the My Clippings.txt document is laid out in date order, so it should be quick and easy to find the particular part of the document you need – your most recently added highlights, bookmarks and clippings will be at the end

Highlights

If you've recently saved a highlight from your favourite book, you can access it here and share it with friends or colleagues by copying and pasting it into an email, or as a social networking update

Clippings

If you've saved a newspaper or magazine article on your Kindle you can access it here. Perhaps you'd like to email it to a friend to read, or append it to a work or school project

---

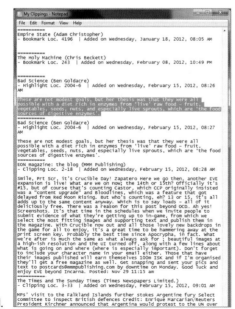

03: Copy and edit

Scroll through the documents folder until you find the file marked My Clippings. You can double-click this file to open it to start editing, or you could copy the whole document to your computer leaving the original intact and unedited.

04: Disconnect your Kindle

Once you've finished copying or editing passages from your My Clippings document you should save your changes, close any text editing applications you've been using and then safely remove (or eject) your Kindle as you would any other USB storage device.

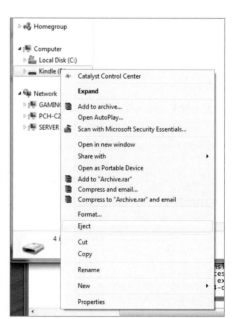

The next step

View Popular Highlights

Want to know what other Kindle readers considered the best bits of the book you're reading? It's easy using Popular Highlights…

Highlights is a little-known feature of the Kindle that enables the user to highlight text within a Kindle book, just like you would use a highlighter pen to do it in a traditional paperback. Not only will phrases and passages you highlight appear underlined as you read your books, but they're also copied and stored in the My Clippings file for quick and easy future reference.

Popular Highlights is a very clever variation on the standard Highlights feature that uses anonymous Highlights information gathered by all the readers of a particular book to highlight the most popular parts, merge them together, and display them on your Kindle.

Not only is this a great mechanism to ensure the very best passages, salient plot points and ideas are brought to your attention, but for academic readers it can be a truly indispensable tool to help ensure the most important information and detail can be focused upon and hopefully retained.

Not only does Amazon ensure the most regularly highlighted passages from across a book's readership is brought to your attention, but you can even see the total number of people who have highlighted that particular section of text. Here's how to start making use of this excellent feature which works almost the same way regardless of whether you're using the Kindle Keyboard or Kindle 4.

"It's a very clever variation on the standard Highlights feature"

01: Get online
Highlights are stored on Amazon's servers, so to view them you'll need to connect your Kindle to the internet first. If you have a 3G model it's easy, for Wi-Fi-only users simply click the Menu button and select the Turn Wireless On option.

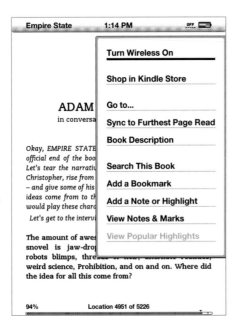

02: Update Popular Highlights
Since readers make new Highlights all the time it's wise to ensure your Kindle is up to date with the latest info. To perform the update just press Menu from the Home screen and choose Sync & Check for Items from the list.

Popular Highlights explained

Here's how this clever feature works…

The device screen (top)

Showing 10 Popular H

Location 1908
Before all masters, r
to, and who teaches
   When the hea

Location 104
William of Orange
undertake and per
success." Cyrus Har

Location 6710
   So is man's hea
which will endure, w
of his superiority ov

Location 2124
an energetic man wi
would vegetate and i
   Herbert distingu

Location 932
   "Better to put things at the worst at first," replied
the engineer, "and reserve the best for a surprise."
   "Well said," remarked Pencroft. "It is to be hoped,

Page 1 of 2   (Close Popular Highlights)

Menu overlay

Turn Wireless Off

Shop in Kindle Store

Go to...

Sync to Furthest Page Read

Book Description

Search This Book

Add a Bookmark

Add a Note or Highlight

View Notes & Marks

View Popular Highlights

Callout boxes

Sync your Kindle
You can't view up-to-date Popular Highlights unless you have a connection to the internet (either via 3G or wireless). Make sure you periodically update the data

Back to the book
With Popular Highlights enabled you can also read the book as usual, but still see the Popular Highlights as you happen across them. What's more, you can also see how many readers have highlighted a particular passage

HOW MANY HIGHLIGHTS?
Not only can you pivot Popular Highlights by popularity or the location within the book that they appear, you can also see exactly how many people have highlighted a particular passage in a book. To view the number of Popular Highlights, simply read your book normally (with Popular Highlights activated) and press the Return (arrow) key to view and hide the details.

Location, location
While you're viewing Popular Highlights they're shown in order of popularity first, while listing the location number they appear. You can also pivot this list to show in location order too

Finishing up
Once you've seen enough, you can close Popular Highlights by scrolling right to the bottom of the screen and clicking the button marked 'Close Popular Highlights'

03: Enable Popular Highlights

While you're reading your book you now simply need to press the Menu button and select the View Popular Highlights option. The list is sorted by the Highlights popularity by default, but using the Menu button you can sort them by book location as well.

strictly guarded, that escape appeared impossible. In the meanwhile Captain Harding was rejoined by a servant who was devoted to him in life and in death. This intrepid fellow was a Negro born on the engineer's estate, of a slave father and mother, but to whom Cyrus, who was an Abolitionist from conviction and heart, had long since given his freedom.
The once slave, though free, would not leave his master. He would have died for him. He was a man of about thirty, vigorous, active, clever, intelligent, gentle, and calm, sometimes naive, always merry, obliging, and honest. His name was Nebuchadnezzar, but he only answered to the familiar abbreviation of Neb.
   When Neb heard that his master had been made prisoner, he left Massachusetts without hesitating an instant, arrived before Richmond, and by dint of stratagem and shrewdness, after having risked his life twenty times over, managed to penetrate into the besieged town. The pleasure of Harding on seeing his servant, and the joy of Neb at finding his master, can scarcely be described.
   But though Neb had been able to make his way into Richmond, it was quite another thing to get out again, for the Northern prisoners were very strictly watched. Some extraordinary opportunity was needed to make the attempt with any chance of success, and this opportunity not only did not present itself, but was very difficult to find.

Press ↵ to show number of highlighters

04: Hiding Popular Highlights

Once you've finished perusing Popular Highlights you can scroll down to the Close Popular Highlights option at the bottom of the page. Don't forget to periodically sync your Kindle to keep the Highlights fresh.

Second device screen

Showing 10 Popular Highlights	By Most Popular

Location 1908   **60 Highlighters**
Before all masters, necessity is the one most listened to, and who teaches the best.
   When the heap of pyrites had been entirely

Location 104   **54 Highlighters**
William of Orange in the 17th century: "I can undertake and persevere even without hope of success." Cyrus Harding was courage personified. He

Location 6710   **52 Highlighters**
   So is man's heart. The desire to perform a work which will endure, which will survive him, is the origin of his superiority over all other living creatures here

Location 2124   **49 Highlighters**
an energetic man will succeed where an indolent one would vegetate and inevitably perish.
   Herbert distinguished himself in these works. He

Location 932   **44 Highlighters**
   "Better to put things at the worst at first," replied the engineer, "and reserve the best for a surprise."
   "Well said," remarked Pencroft. "It is to be hoped,

Page 1 of 2   (Close Popular Highlights)

Make the most of Public Notes

Find out what your friends think of your favourite books
with one of the best social tools Kindle has to offer…

Besides Popular Highlights, Public Notes is one of the most useful and addictive parts of the Kindle's social networking capabilities. The idea is straightforward – you 'follow' other Kindle users from its sizeable user base at **kindle.amazon.com**, then, when someone you follow highlights or adds a note to a particular passage in a book you're reading your Kindle will automatically highlight the same passage.

The name of the highlighter is displayed alongside the highlighted passage, and assuming they also make a note, an '@' symbol will appear by the passage so you can view the note they've made.

Not only will Public Notes be automatically displayed while you read, but they also appear in the same list as your own personal annotations provided you select the View Notes & Marks option using the Menu button. What's more, the feature is enabled by default, making it really easy to start making use of it. That said, it's easy to turn off the feature in the Settings option. Public Notes are only compatible with books and don't work with magazines or newspapers, but the feature works much the same way whether you're reading via the 3G or 4th generation Kindle.

"Public Notes are only compatible with books and don't work with magazines"

01: Follow friends or personalities
Before you start using Public Notes, you need to be following a few people that enjoy the same books as you. Access **kindle.amazon.com**, sign in and then search for books or people and select Follow.

02: Connect to the internet
You need to be online to make use of Public Notes on your Kindle. To enable Wi-Fi, simply press the Menu button (from the Home screen, or from within a book) and select the top option – Turn Wireless On.

Following friends and personalities

Follow users to access their Public Notes via kindle.amazon.com

Signing in
Click on the small downward-facing arrow in the top-left corner of the page to sign in to your Kindle account

Your public stats
Once you've started following, accruing followers and making Public Notes, your stats are displayed here. You can also find people you know using the Twitter and Facebook buttons just below

Search for books and people
You can use the search bar to search for people or books you're interested in. Once you've found people who are reading the same books as you, you can click Follow from their profile page

Highly followed people
The Kindle website automatically shows a selection of personalities that already have a good number of followers and Public Notes. Click their picture to view their profile to see what they're reading and making notes on

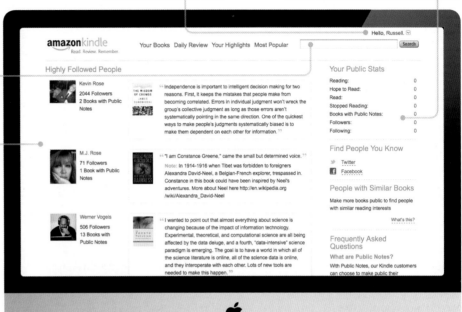

THE MOST PUBLIC NOTES
Instead of hoping for pot luck that someone whose opinion you respect has made a Public Note in a book you'd like to read, you can view individual readers' collections to see what books they've made notes on via the **kindle.amazon.com** website. It's also possible to view a list of the most regularly noted books on the website too.

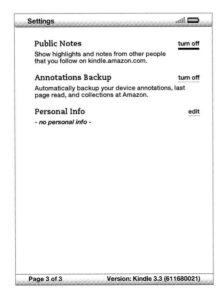

03: Turn on Public Notes
From the Home screen, press the Menu button and then select Settings. Using your page-turning buttons scroll down through the options until you find the setting called Public Notes. Highlight it with your five-way controller and select it to turn it on. You can turn it off in exactly the same way.

04: Using Public Notes
Ensure you sync your Kindle by selecting Menu from the Home screen and choosing Sync & Check for Items, then open a book you know a friend or personality has made Public Notes in. If you want to skip straight to their notes, simply select the View Notes & Marks option using the Menu button while reading.

Share your activity on social networking sites

What better way to strike up reading-related conversation with your friends and relatives than to share your Kindle exploits through your social network sites?

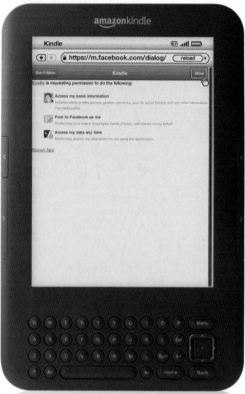

One of the most immediate ways to connect with friends and colleagues using your Kindle is to share your notes and highlights with them via the world's most popular social networking sites – Twitter and Facebook. Connecting your Kindle account with your social media accounts is really quite straightforward, and once you've configured the required settings, sharing passages from the book you're reading or notes you've made about them, is even easier still.

All it takes is a quick trip to the Settings section – so you simply right-click the Menu button from the Home Screen and select Settings. Once there, tab the pages down until you find 'Social Networks' and

click Manage to associate your Twitter and/ or Facebook account to your Kindle one.

Once you're all up and running, you can then tweet or update your status from your Kindle whenever you want with the press of a button. Not only can you highlight passages to share as part of your post, but you can also access your Clippings document to talk about passages or notes you've previously made.

One word of warning though. By default the Kindle is set up to automatically tweet or update your status whenever you finish a book (which isn't the most interesting of status updates). If you're not keen on the Kindle posting for you, not to worry – in the following guide we also break down how to disable this feature.

Making a social media update
Posting to Twitter & Facebook at a glance

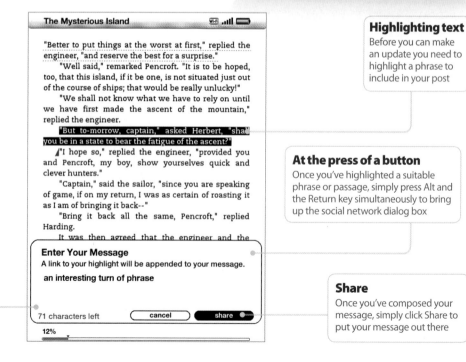

100 characters or less
Since Twitter puts a limit on the number of characters you can Tweet in one go, you only have 100 characters to play with

Highlighting text
Before you can make an update you need to highlight a phrase to include in your post

At the press of a button
Once you've highlighted a suitable phrase or passage, simply press Alt and the Return key simultaneously to bring up the social network dialog box

Share
Once you've composed your message, simply click Share to put your message out there

01: Turn on Wi-Fi

Assuming you're not using a 3G-enabled Kindle device you'll need to enable your Wi-Fi access to make use of its social networking capabilities. Just click the Menu button from the Home screen and select Turn Wireless On. Once you're connected to a suitable network you can continue to the next step.

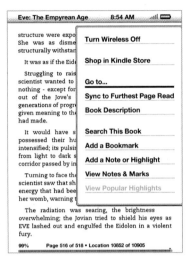

02: Managing your social networks

From the Home screen click Menu, then select Settings. From here, page down to the option called Social Networks and click the Manage button. You'll see two options – one to link a Twitter account, the other to Link to Facebook.

03: Connecting your accounts

To connect to your accounts click one of the links and input your username and password. Once you've agreed to the conditions you'll see that your account username appears above a new option to unlink your account. Repeat the process for your second social networking account if you have one.

04: Making an update

While you're reading a book, highlight a passage of text by clicking the button in the five-way controller and move the cursor to make your highlight. Now click the Alt and Return keys simultaneously to call up the social networking dialog box and enter a 100-character message. When you're ready, simply click Share to make your update.

05: Sharing from My Clippings

If you're unable to connect to the internet at the time you highlight a passage you can save it to your My Clippings file for a later social media update. Once you have an Internet connection again, simply access My Clippings from the Home Screen (listed among your books) and highlight the passage from there. Click Alt and Return simultaneously and make you update, as previously shown.

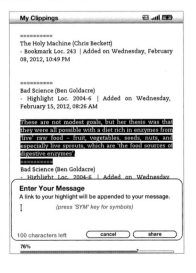

06: Disabling auto updates

If you don't want your Kindle to update your Twitter or Facebook status all by itself, then we recommend you visit **kindle.amazon.com** and select Preferences from the top right corner of the screen. Under the Twitter and Facebook section of the page there is a small tick box for each – ensure this is unticked and no updates will be made without your knowledge.

Use a gift certificate

Gift certificates are a great way to give eBooks as presents – and they're easier to redeem than you might think

Ever since portable digital devices got the ability to hold downloadable content, companies like Apple and Amazon have been making it easier and easier for us to buy content from their online stores.

It's a no-brainer – make it as easy as possible for people to buy and download, and they'll be much more likely to do so. It's simple for someone to buy a gift certificate online from Amazon and then have it emailed to you.

Next, go to the Kindle store or Amazon bookstore on your computer and find a book to download. When you get to the checkout stage, enter the promotional code that you were sent along with the certificate. This applies a discount to your order in the amount shown on the certificate, and any extra money due will be billed to your payment card. The book will then become available in your Amazon account and accessible from your Kindle or Amazon devices.

The great thing about gift certificates is that they are sent by email, so even if someone is on the other side of the word, they can receive your gift and redeem it straight away. Additionally, thanks to everything being tied into your Amazon account, your purchases will be available on all your devices. It's a great way to give and receive books.

"Your purchases will be available on all your devices"

01: Redeem the code

Click on the 'Redeem' link in the email, and you will be prompted to sign into your Amazon account. Click 'Apply To Your Account'.

02: Go to the store

Go to the Kindle Store and sign in as you would normally. Then, find a book to buy and add it to your cart.

Redeeming a gift for Kindle

A few clicks is all it takes to use your Amazon gift certificate

Claim code
A unique code that you use to redeem your gift. You don't need to remember this, but it's handy to have in case of any problems

Redeem now
Click this button to be taken through the sign-in process to your Amazon account. You will then be able to apply the gift amount to your Amazon account

EXTRA MONEY
If the amount in the gift certificate doesn't cover the cost of the item you want to buy, then you can apply it and the remaining balance will be automatically paid by the card that you already have set up on your Amazon account.

The amount
The all-important amount that lets you know how much you'll be able to spend on your gift. Many eBooks are very inexpensive

Apply to Account
Click on this link and you will be taken directly to the part of the site where you apply the funds. This is the quickest possible way to get through the whole process

03: Choose a device
After clicking 'Buy', you can choose which device you would like the book to be delivered wirelessly to.

04: Read on Kindle
The book will be wirelessly pushed to whichever device you selected. Go to the home screen on your Kindle, and it should be there and available to read almost instantly.

Get online with your Kindle

We reveal how you can take your new Kindle online to surf the internet and find anything that interests you

One of the more useful applications of the Kindle is its ability to go online and browse the internet. It's worth remembering, though, that at its best (on third-generation Kindles) it is a limited way of surfing the web, and at its worst (on fourth-generation Kindles without a physical keyboard), it's an extremely cumbersome one as well.

The Kindle is an eReader first and foremost, and while it's commendable that Amazon has allowed you to browse the internet, which in itself can be extremely handy, it's worth noting that there will be many things that you won't be able to view that you would normally take for granted when surfing online. If you're expecting to watch YouTube videos, play Flash games

or plan your local Tesco shop, you're going to be disappointed. If, however, you simply want to read the latest news stories or find out what's happening on your favourite websites, you won't be disappointed.

The following walkthrough will show you how to do everything from logging on to the internet, to saving bookmarks, entering a URL, downloading files and much more. These handy tips work on both versions of the Kindle, but it's worth noting that any references to typing in words on the keyboard will be referring to the virtual keyboard that appears on the fourth-generation Kindle.

So join us over the following 12 steps and you'll never be stumped again when taking your Kindle online.

"You'll never be stumped again when taking your Kindle online"

Web Browser – the basics

A simple guide to the average Kindle web page

Zooming in

This box can be moved around the screen at will with the five-way controller. Activate the controller's middle button to zoom in. This allows you to read the page more easily

MORE BOOKS

The Kindle has access to a huge number of books, but it never hurts to have even more – especially free ones. If you're looking for alternatives to Amazon's store, then why not consider a website like www.mobipocket. com? It has access to thousands of books (and many free ones) that can be immediately downloaded to your Home screen.

Entering URLs

This is where the website addresses you enter are shown. You can view any websites, but some might not properly display, if they rely on things like Flash to work

Reload a site

Sometimes a website will hang and you can be waiting forever for it to load. Solve the problem by navigating to this button with the five-way controller and clicking it

01: Getting started

Turn your Kindle on and then press the Menu button. This will bring up a drop-down list that lets you do everything from shop in the Kindle Store to changing settings. Turn your wireless settings on (if needed), then use the five-way controller to select Experimental. Once selected, press the middle button on the controller.

02: Getting online

You are now on the Experimental page of your Kindle. If you are using a Kindle third generation, this page also includes Play MP3 and Text-To-Speech options. If you have a fourth generation Kindle you will just see Web Browser as an option. Navigate down to Web Browser and then select the 'launch browser' option.

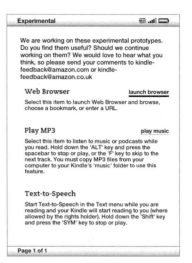

03: Entering a URL

You should now be on a bookmark page with useful websites like Amazon, Wikipedia and Google. If there is a specific website you wish to visit, simply press the Menu button, go to Enter URL using the five-way controller and then type the URL of the website you wish to visit. Press Enter to be taken there.

04: Adding bookmarks

When you find a website you like the look of you can bookmark it, so that you can easily return to it at a later date. To bookmark a page, you'll need to open up the menu again and head down to Bookmark This Page. Press the middle button on your five-way controller to add it to the rest of your bookmarks.

05: Editing/ deleting bookmarks

Press the Menu button and navigate to Bookmarks. You will now see a list of all your saved bookmarks. If you want to edit the name of a bookmark to make it more recognisable, select the site in question and press right on the five-way controller. If you wish to delete the bookmark, press left instead.

06: Zooming in

If you're having trouble reading small text, this can be easily changed. When entering a new page you will see a transparent box with a magnifying glass on it. Move this around with the five-way controller then press the centre button to zoom in. Press the Menu button and select Zoom Out to return to the full page.

The next step

07: Navigating large pages

Some pages can be extremely long, with lots on information on them to find. You can easily navigate to the top and bottom of a page by using your Kindle's Next Page and Previous Page buttons. Alternatively, if you want to be more specific, you can use the five-way controller. It's slower, but more accurate.

08: Selecting links, buttons and boxes

Using website links, entering text in boxes or just ticking required buttons while online is extremely easy. Just use the five-way controller to select the link or box in question, then press the middle button to select. You'll be either taken to a new page, or can write out the required text with your keyboard.

09: Using History

Sometimes you'll realise that you want to visit a page that you've previously looked at. The easiest way to do this is to press the Menu button, scroll down to History with the five-way controller and select it. You'll now see all the pages you've ever visited. Just select the one you want.

10: Downloading files

It's possible to download certain files to view from your Home screen. Simply select the file you wish to download with the five-way controller and follow the on-screen instructions. You can download files ending in AZW, AZW1 (Kindle), MOBI, PRC (unprotected Mobipocket Books) and text files that end in TXT.

11: Browser Settings

Sometimes you'll want to make additional changes, like clearing cookies, making pages faster to read, or simply clearing your history. To do this, press the Menu button and navigate down to Browser Settings. You can then do the following: Clear History, Clear Cookies, Disable Javascript or Disable Images. Simply navigate to Close Settings to leave the menu.

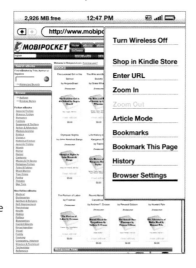

12: Article Mode

Article Mode can be very useful as it effectively cuts out all of the extraneous stuff found on a page and just displays the actual web content. In order to use this useful mode, press the Menu button and navigate down to Article Mode. Select and you're all ready to go.

Instant web guide

Everything you need to know to browse the web

Entering URLs
This couldn't be easier. Simply navigate to the Enter URL option with the five-way controller and click the middle button. Then you just type in the website address

Zoom In/Out
You can't zoom out effectively from the main page, so you'll need to visit this part of the menu instead. You can also zoom in here, but it takes longer

Bookmark a page
Sometimes you'll want to save a webpage for future reference. When you do, select this menu option to save a page. Very handy!

Bookmarks
When you navigate to and click on this particular part of the menu, you'll immediately be taken to everything you've ever bookmarked. Very handy for finding favourite sites in a hurry

Article Mode
If all you want to do is look at web pages in their raw form, then this is what you need to select. It's very useful as websites load that little bit faster

History
Have you ever been in a situation when you wanted to return to a website, but couldn't remember what it was? Bring up History and you'll be able to find anything you've looked at

Settings control
The Browser Settings are very useful. In addition to letting you clear history and cookies, you can also disable JavaScript and images

---

Alternative eBook sites More sites to get your eBook fix from

Smashwords
www.smashwords.com
Smashwords has plenty of books available for Kindle. Its emphasis on independent work means you'll find books here that you won't find anywhere else.

Manybooks
www.manybooks.net
As one of the leading provider of public domain books, Manybooks has plenty to offer Kindle users – all for free!

Feedbooks
www.feedbooks.com
Feedbooks offers a collection of original eBooks and public domain works. It stocks large fiction and non-fiction collections.

Pixel of Ink
www.pixelofink.com
Rather than host any eBooks itself, Pixel of Ink keeps readers informed of any daily deals currently available on the Kindle Store.

Free Kindle Books
freekindlebooks.org
The website might look a bit basic, but Free Kindle Books offers a comprehensive selection of free eBooks already in .mobi format.

Play games on your Kindle

There are two hidden games on your Kindle which will while away the time in between reading. We show you how to find them

There is no getting away from games. And why should there be? They're fun and give you a welcome breather, which is why we were pleased to see a couple hidden on the Kindle.

While they are not of the standard of *Call Of Duty*, these freebies were introduced in the autumn of 2010 when Kindle Keyboard was released, allowing users of the device to play a strategy game called *GoMoku* and the old favourite *Minesweeper*. They aren't playable on Kindle 4s.

The games are a bit hidden in Kindle menus, however. Indeed, you won't find them mentioned in any of the help topics nor will you see a menu linking to them. They are, rather cutely, referred to as Easter Eggs – a little present for users to find.

But even though the games are free and hidden from view, that doesn't mean care and attention hasn't been lavished upon them. The control systems are good for both games and, in the case of *GoMoku*, the Kindle proves to be more than a good opponent.

It shows the potential of the Kindle as an all-round entertainment device and there are more titles out there including *Shuffled Row* and *Every Word*. If you don't mind paying for games, then it's worth giving *Scrabble* a try. Note that these are not available in the UK.

All of the games are in black and white, but the bonus is that playing them for hours on end won't hurt your eyes. And that's got to be a good thing.

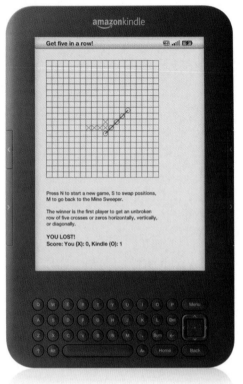

"It shows the potential of the Kindle as an all-round entertainment device"

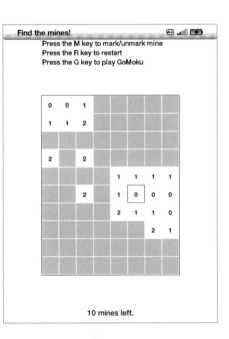

01: Access the games

To start playing games on your Kindle, hold down Shift+Alt+M. This will call up *Minesweeper*. Use the four-way controller to move around the grid and click the centre button to expose a cell. Press 'M' to make a grid square you think contains a mine.

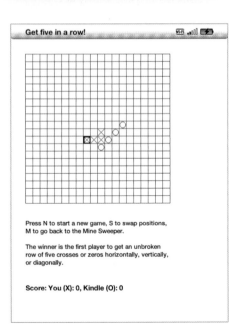

02: Access GoMoku

If you get bored of *Minesweeper*, then you can try another game. Press 'G' and *GoMoku* appears. This is the same game as Five in a Row and it's similar to noughts and crosses requiring a strategical brain. The Kindle plays a mean game!

Playing Minesweeper

Getting into the hidden gems

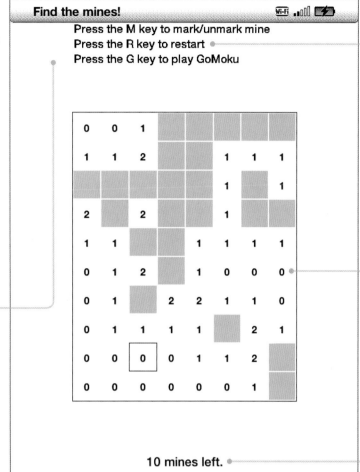

Find the mines!

Press the M key to mark/unmark mine
Press the R key to restart
Press the G key to play GoMoku

10 mines left.

Restart a game
If you feel it's time to start again, just press 'R' and you can to go back to the beginning for another go

Main screen
Use the cursor to move around the playing area, pressing 'M' to indicate where you think a mine should be, looking at the numbers for clues

How many left?
The number of mines in a game is shown at the bottom. The idea is that you locate them all and sweep the board of potential bombs

Play another
If you want to play *GoMoku*, just press 'G' as indicated at the top of the screen. Your game of *Minesweeper* will be saved for later

KINDLE FIRE
It appears that games are very much on the Amazon agenda, in particular when it comes to the Kindle Fire. This colour device has a vast array of games already, taking advantage of a screen that is better enabled for fast-paced, graphically intensive offerings. *Angry Birds* is on there already.

03: Other games
Games are available to buy or download for free on the US Amazon Store, but not in the UK at the moment. Here you can grab titles like *Scrabble*, *Thread Words* and *Shuffled Row*. There is also an updated *Minesweeper*, but you may want something new.

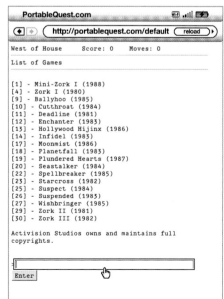

04: Web games
There are some web games that you can play no matter what country you are in as long as you have an internet connection. Try one of the brilliant classic text adventure games that have been optimised for Kindle at **portablequest.com**.

The next step

Send personal documents to your Kindle

Wirelessly send documents to your Kindle and view them at any time, saving you loads of paper in the process

The Kindle is built for text so it's good to know that you're not restricted to reading pre-prepared books. Using the Kindle Personal Documents service, you and other people can send personal documents straight to your device.

Everyone who registers a Kindle is given a unique email address, which ends in @kindle.com. This provides a fast and efficient way of transferring files up to 50MB. You can send a range of files including Word (.doc and .docx), HTML, Rich Text Format (.rtf) and Kindle Format (.mobi and .azw). You can also send images as .jpeg, .jpg, .gif, .png and .bmp. PDFs are accepted, but may require conversion.

To protect your Kindle from being bombarded with files, you have to approve the sender of a document. It's not possible to send more than 25 documents at once and you can't send documents to more than 15 Send-to-Kindle email addresses.

Documents are automatically archived. These will remain in your Kindle library until they are deleted. One of the nice features of being able to read your own documents is that they are treated in the same way as books. Your last page read is stored and you can make annotations or bookmark parts. It makes using the Kindle a whole lot neater than printing your documents.

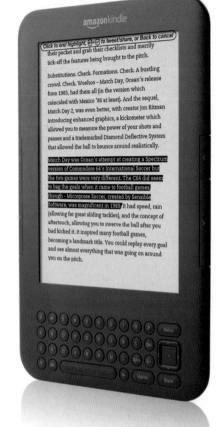

"Everyone who registers a Kindle is given a unique email address"

01: Send-to-Kindle email

When you register your Kindle, you are assigned an email address for your device. You can send documents to this address. If you are unsure what your address is, you can find it under Settings (press the Menu button).

02: Create an email

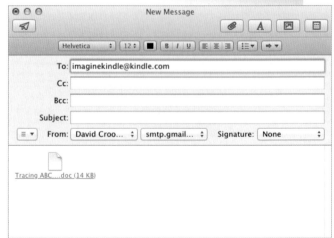

Go to your email client and create a new email. Attach the file you wish to send to your Kindle. You don't need to include a subject. Just make sure you input the Kindle's email address in the To field.

Work with your document

How to make notes on your documents

Highlight
Words can be highlighted to either tweet or share. Just click to start making a highlight and then use the cursor to define the extent of the highlight

WHISPERSYNC
The Whispersync function synchronises your last page read, bookmarks and annotations for all of your documents except PDFs. But it only works when you send your documents via your Send-to-Kindle e-mail because this converts files into Kindle format. It won't work via USB transfers or unconverted PDFs. You also need the Kindle 3.3 software on your device.

Annotate
Select an area of your document and start to type. A box will appear. You can save your note for later reference and the Kindle responds by numbering each annotation

Define words
You can also find out the definitions of certain words by clicking on them. The definition will appear at either the top or bottom of the screen

Change address
The documents are sent to your Kindle email address. You can edit the address or create additional ones at **amazon. co.uk/myk**

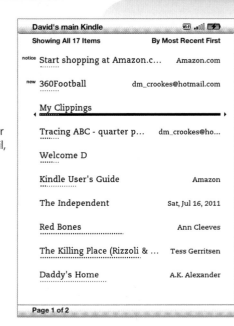

Begin typing to create a note or click to start a highlight
game 1 n. 1 a form of play or sport, esp. a competitive one played according to rules and   **more ⊕**

EA's Canadian team, British gamers took FIFA to their hearts and it became available on a host of consoles and computers including the Amiga, Sega Master System, Mega CD, Game Gear, SNES, 3DO and Game Boy.

But it wasn't alone. A year earlier – in 1992 – Konami produced Hyper Soccer on the NES. That game was the effective precursor of the Pro-Evo games. So when EA introduced FIFA, it sowed the seeds of Manchester United/Chelsea style battle that would rage for close to two decades. And just like those two real-life teams over the past decade, both games have found themselves winning the league in various years. It's only recently that FIFA has started to waltz away with the European Cup.

To see how FIFA and Pro-Evo got this far, it's time to go back in time to the days when footballers earned two bob a week and tackles were fearlessly hard. We're going to rewind to the days of standing on the terraces munching meat pies before prawn sandwiches were invented. Yeah, those days when Liverpool FC dominated, hooliganism was rife and players had to
23%

03: Send it
Press Send. In order to receive the email, the sender's email will need to be approved. Follow the steps in our relevant tutorial for this (page 132). When the document arrives it will state Items Downloaded. The doc will say New next to it.

David's main Kindle

Showing All 17 Items   By Most Recent First

notice Start shopping at Amazon.c...   Amazon.com

new 360Football   dm_crookes@hotmail.com

◄ My Clippings   ►

Tracing ABC - quarter p...   dm_crookes@ho...

Welcome D

Kindle User's Guide   Amazon

The Independent   Sat, Jul 16, 2011

Red Bones   Ann Cleeves

The Killing Place (Rizzoli & ...   Tess Gerritsen

Daddy's Home   A.K. Alexander

Page 1 of 2

04: Converted document
Your document will have been converted into a format that the Kindle can work with. Open your document and you can make annotated notes by going to the relevant place, selecting it and using the pop-up text entry window.

[app icon]
ICON_(tracingABC)

[review body – 80 words/approx 450 characters including spaces. Please stick to word counts, otherwise the work will be sent back to you]
Learning how to write is still a major skill, despite a world of keyboards. Tracing ABE allows young people to become familiar with the alphabet, tracing their fingers on each of the 26 letters in both upper and lower case. There are numbers too. Aimed at children aged four and up, the app presents itself as a game to make learning fun. In time, it hopes to add full-word tracing. As it stands, however, it's a valuable tool.

you can make notes

(cancel) (clear) (save & share) (save note) ►
52%

The next step

Set up and delete approved
contacts
Ensure you or someone you know and trust can send documents to your Kindle by approving them beforehand

It's possible for other people to send personal documents to your Kindle. All they need is your special Kindle email address, which you receive when you register your device. But knowing this alone does not open up the floodgates. That is, if your Kindle email found its way into the wrong hands, you are not going to suddenly be bombarded with spam.

That's because, in order for someone to send you a document, you have to approve your contact. The same goes for your own

email address. You can only send items to your Kindle from an address that you have given the go-ahead to.

All of this is managed online using the special area created on the Amazon website for this purpose. On these pages we show you how to navigate to that site and make amends. We also highlight how you can not only create but delete contacts too, which is handy if you change your email address or if somebody you approved needs to be blocked.

This area of the Amazon website can also be used to change the email address of your Kindle. Pressing Edit next to your Kindle's email address will allow you to alter it to something else. You could, for extra security, alter this to one that is complicated, but the measures adopted by Amazon will ensure that your Kindle is suitably out of the way of undesirables while also making it very easy for you to transfer your personal documents. And to find out how to do that, check out our tutorial on page 130.

Understanding the settings
Find your way around the Manage Your Kindle screen

Send-to-Kindle
You can change your Kindle email address. This is the address to which personal documents will be sent via any contacts that you have approved

Approving people
This area shows all of the email addresses that you have approved as senders for your Kindle. If an email address is not listed here, it cannot be used to send a document

Website
You can only manage your Kindle settings via the website, which you can get to via the left-hand menu on Amazon

Information
When a new email address is added, a notification is added in green so that you can instantly see what has just happened. Deleting addresses will make them immediately disappear

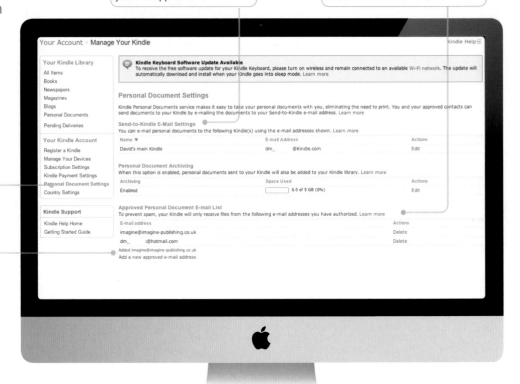

01: Manage your Kindle

Go to Amazon and, in the left-hand menu, select Kindle. Scroll down to Manage Your Kindle. You will be asked to sign in using your Amazon account and this will take you into the administration area.

02: Personal Document Settings

On the left-hand menu, under Your Kindle Account, you will see an option for Personal Document Settings. Click on this. We're going to be approving the personal document email list.

03: Approved email list

Scroll down to Approved Personal Document Email List. Under here you should see the email you used when registering your Kindle. You have to approve emails to prevent yourself from spam.

04: Add a new address

To create an additional approved personal document email, click 'Add a new approved e-mail address'. A box will appear. Simply type the email address in here.

05: Deleting an address

If you need to remove an email address, go to the email address you wish to remove and click Delete. You will not be asked if you want to confirm this. The address will go as soon as you click Delete.

06: Tell your friend

If you have added a friend's or colleague's email address, all you have to do is let them know. They can then send you an email with an attached document and be sure that you will be able to receive it.

Read PDFs on your Kindle

PDFs are used everywhere these days, and you can send them to the Kindle and read them like a book!

It's possible, and simple, to read the popular PDF format on your Kindle. Your device has a built-in Adobe PDF reader and this means you can import a file without losing any of the original formatting and since the PDF standard is used worldwide – such documents can be read by practically any computer or device – being able to use them on a Kindle opens up a host of possibilities for you.

The PDF reader allows you to magnify your documents. Using the Text (Aa) key, you can select how much you want to zoom. You can flip back and forth using the usual buttons left and right too.

And yet, because the screen is small, you may find the need to keep zooming becomes annoying. The text of the PDF is likely to be small and difficult to read because it won't have been created with a six-inch screen in mind. The zoom feature of the PDF reader is also quite fiddly. It breaks your document into chunks and so it means reading a PDF is not the most fluid of experiences.

To make reading PDFs easier, convert them into the Kindle format. This will give you a continuous text document which can be manipulated and read in the same way as a normal Kindle book.

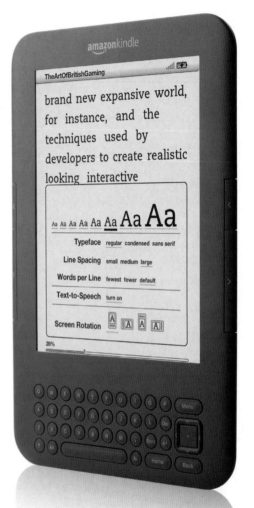

"To make reading PDFs easier, convert them into the Kindle format"

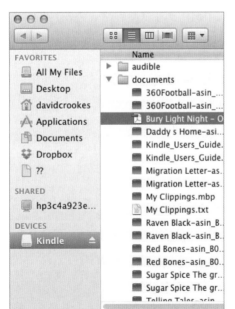

01: Plug in USB

Plug your Kindle into your computer using the USB lead. The Kindle will show on your computer. Click on it and navigate to the Documents folder. Simply find a PDF on your computer and copy it into this folder. Then Eject your Kindle.

02: Send a PDF

Alternatively, you can send a PDF from an email address. Find out what your device's Kindle address is (it's under settings). Now send an email with your PDF attached to your Kindle address. As in our first step, the PDF will appear on your Kindle.

Reading PDFs on a Kindle

We look at the tricks of PDF reading

Move pages
You can move back and forth from page to page by using the left and right buttons, just as you would when reading any book or document on your Kindle

Zoom
You have three zooming options when reading a PDF on a Kindle. You can zoom at 150%, 200% or 300%. Press 'Aa' to get these options

Lighten up
PDFs can be lightened or darkened depending on your preference and this can be good if there are images. Again, press Aa. Choose from lightest through to darkest

Change the resolution
PDFs can look better when the screen is flipped so that you are viewing in landscape rather than portrait mode. Press 'Aa' and make your selection

LANDSCAPE MODE
If you find that the display of an original PDF is not quite right, then you can switch it from portrait to landscape mode by pressing the Text button (Aa). By rotating the screen in this way, small fonts become more readable and there is less panning to be done, ensuring reading an unconverted PDF is more pleasurable.

03: Reading a PDF
Click on your PDF and it will be displayed on your Kindle. Use the left and right buttons to scroll through the pages. To zoom, press Aa and select the Zoom option. A box will appear and you can choose which part of the screen to enlarge.

04: Convert a PDF
If you want your PDF to be converted into the Kindle format, then when you send an email to your Kindle address, make sure you put the word 'convert' in the subject line. Then when the PDF is received by the Kindle it will look like a normal book.

brand new expansive world, for instance, and the techniques used by developers to create realistic looking interactive landscapes that employ shadows, light effects and physics.

We would explore the uncanny valley – the pitfall of creating human-like faces and why they can often have a zombie effect – and

View images on your Kindle

Although the Kindle is geared up to showcase text, you can still use it as a nifty black-and-white image viewer

In many ways, your Kindle is a mini computer, albeit a limited one. You can obviously read and this is its greatest function, displaying text without straining your eyes using its famous e-ink technology. But being able to view monochrome images can come in useful too, especially so if you are a major fan of black-and-white photography or if you have some visual documents which you want to carry around.

The image viewer is not an obvious feature. That is, you won't be able to find a direct link to it from the home page. To access it, you have to do a little bit of trickery, but it's not difficult and nor will it involve damaging your machine. It's a simple case of plugging your Kindle into

your computer, be it a PC or Mac, opening it up and creating a new folder. Produce sub-folders and then throw your images into them. When you unplug your Kindle, all of your images will be there ready and waiting for you to use.

It's such a handy addition to the Kindle feature set and it was introduced with the Kindle 3 operating system. Quite why more isn't made of it, we're not too sure, but we're glad it's included all the same. It also means that your Kindle can double up as an effective USB drive – there is nothing to stop you plugging your Kindle into a different computer and copying the files off it. And that goes for any sort of file, making your Kindle even more of an essential purchase.

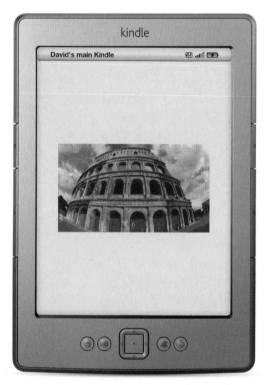

"Being able to view monochrome images can come in useful"

01: Plug in Kindle

In order to get images on to your Kindle, you need to have it plugged in. Use your USB lead and then find your Kindle on your PC or Mac desktop and double-click on it. It will appear as a removable drive.

02: Create a pictures folder

You need to create a pictures folder in the root directory. This is the one that also holds the 'audible', 'documents' and 'music' folders. Right-click and select New Folder. Name it 'pictures' and press Enter in order to confirm it.

Working with images

An in-depth look at the image viewer

Panning
You can move around the image by using the navigation controller. Just tap it in the direction you want to go

Rotate
If you want to flip your image 90 degrees at a time, then keep pressing the 'R' button. This is perfect for seeing more of an image

Use full screen
You can view images using the full Kindle screen by pressing 'F' on the keyboard. This is one of the many keypresses built into the image viewer

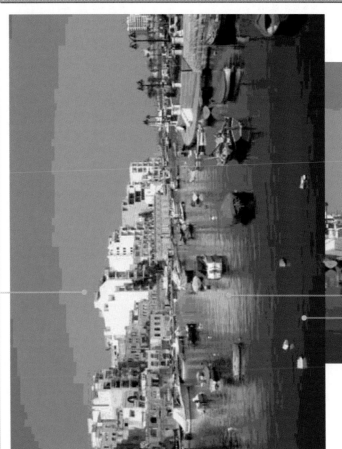

David's main Kindle

MOVE BETWEEN IMAGES
To see each individual image within a collection on your Kindle, you only need to tap the page-turn buttons as you would when reading a book. This lets you go back and forth through your gallery with the greatest of ease.

Zooming
By pressing 'G', you can zoom in on your image and pressing 'W' lets you zoom out. Press 'E' and you can reset the zoom

03: Add images
You need to create a sub-folder, and you can make as many as you wish. Open the 'pictures' folder, right-click and create another New Folder. To add images, find pictures on your computer and drag them in to one of these folders.

04: Unplug the Kindle
Unplug the Kindle and press Alt+Z to refresh. The sub-folders within 'pictures' will show up. Click on the folder and the Image Viewer will launch. Now you can see your pictures in all of their monochrome glory.

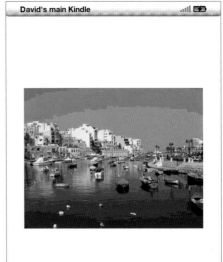

Transfer MP3s to your Kindle

Fancy a little background music while you enjoy your favourite novel? Then use this handy guide to transfer your songs to your new Kindle

The Kindle can store thousands of your favourite books and novels, making it an essential device for those who love reading, but may be short on space. What you might not realise though, is that Amazon's popular device is also capable of storing many other different types of digital media, turning it into quite a versatile, and very useful platform.

In this tutorial we'll be explaining, in six simple steps how you can transfer any number of MP3s to your Kindle device. This will ensure

that you'll always have a way of listening to your favourite tunes, and that reading will never be something you have to do in complete silence. And let's face it, while it's sometimes nice to properly concentrate on a book, a decent bit of background noise can be just as effective as creating atmosphere.

One thing that's worth keeping in mind, is that your Kindle doesn't have an infinite amount of space on it, and that music files are far larger than the average book file. Music files

are measured in megabytes (MB), while book files are in kilobytes (KB) – this is why Kindles are able to store thousands of books on them. You'll still be able to store a large number of MP3 music files on your Kindle, but it's worth remembering that the average Kindle is around 3 gigabytes (approx 3,000MB) in size, which fills up quickly when you start filling it with countless albums. This tutorial is not for use with fourth generation Kindles, as they don't support MP3 playback, unfortunately.

Transfer your files

An in-depth look at transferring MP3s on PC

Albums and singles
Here are your music folders. You can happily transfer across either full albums or single MP3s. Don't worry as your Kindle will be able to select them regardless of their type

Your Kindle folder
This is your Kindle's 'Music' folder. This folder is where you keep all the songs and music that you wish to transfer across. Make sure you add all of your favourites

Your music files
This folder contains all of your available music and should be full of lots of tracks and albums. If this folder is empty, get some songs from iTunes or transfer some CDs

Closing windows
If you accidentally close down your Kindle window, you can easily get it back. Simply go back down to the Start menu and select My Computer or Computer and select Kindle

"You'll always have a way of listening to your favourite tunes"

01: Get yourself connected

Take the plug off your Kindle lead, which reveals a USB socket. Stick that socket into an available port on your computer to connect. Your computer should now show a small AutoPlay box (on PC).

02: Find your Kindle

Click Start and navigate to My Computer. This will bring up a window with your various drives and connections. You'll find your Kindle here. All you need to do now is simply double-click to open it.

03: Preparing the transfer

Navigate to Music. Double-click on the file in order to open it. If it's not there, simply create one by right-clicking within the window and selecting New Folder. Once created, call it Music.

04: Get your music

Now you need to find some music. This is found in Start>Music, but you may have stored it elsewhere. Once you've found your music files, check that they are in the MP3 format.

05: Transfer the files

Now decide what songs to transfer over to your Kindle. Select the tracks or albums you wish to transfer, right-click and select Copy. Now go to your Kindle's empty Music folder and select Paste.

06: Finishing off

Go through the rest of your collection to get any additional songs. Be sure to not fill your Kindle completely though, as you'll have no room for books. Once you have your songs, safely disconnect your Kindle.

Listen to music on your Kindle

Not everyone wants to read in silence. Here's how to listen to songs while reading on a Kindle Keyboard

There's nothing more satisfying than getting stuck into a book. A good book has the power to totally immerse you within its pages, making it possible to lose track of time as you follow the exploits of your favourite character.

Sometimes though, you might want a change of pace, or you might be reading something on your Kindle that doesn't require such intense concentration, like a magazine or a newspaper. In this case, why not take advantage of the fact that your Kindle can play MP3s and simply listen to some of your favourite music while you read? We've already shown you how to transfer MP3s over to your Kindle, and actually listening to them is even easier. This straightforward tutorial means that

you'll never have to read newspapers, magazines, or your favourite books in silence again, as your favourite songs and albums will only be a few button presses away from you.

One thing to bear in mind though is that the ability to play and listen to MP3s is only actually available on Kindles that support a physical keyboard. Amazon made a number of changes to its current fourth generation kindle, and the loss of MP3s was just one of the things dropped to bring the machine down to a sensible price. Providing you do have the correct Kindle device though, you'll find the following guide to be an incredibly useful way of furthering and enhancing the reading enjoyment you get from a Kindle.

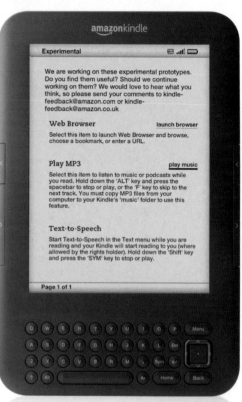

"Simply listen to some of your favourite music while you read"

01: Getting started

Once your Kindle is switched on you need to make sure you're on the Home screen. All you need to do is press the Home button found on your keyboard. Once done you'll be all ready for the next step of the simple process.

Melanies Kindle

Showing 14 Items — By Title

thriller

the basement	Stephen Leather
The Blood That Bonds	Christopher Buecheler
Bloody Valentine	James Patterson
Deeper Water (Tides of Tr...	Robert Whitlow
The Demon Girl (The Ra...	Penelope Fletcher
House of Dark Shadows (...	Robert Liparulo
Mystery	Jonathan Kellerman
once bitten	Stephen Leather
Painless	Derek Ciccone

Page 1 of 2

02: Home sweet home

This is the Home screen, the place where you can find all the core contents of your Kindle. Categories of the different books are kept here. Your next step is to press the Menu button, which is found above your five-way controller.

Melanies Kindle

Showing All 13 Items — By Collections

thriller (14)	
chicklit (11)	
classics (22)	
A Girl Like You (a Donovan Cr...	John Locke
My Clippings	
Welcome darran	
The Unremarkable Heart	Karin Slaughter
Falling Star	Diana Dempsey
A Very Special Delivery	Linda Goodnight
sample An Inconvenient Marriage	Ruth Ann Nordin

Page 1 of 2

Get the most out of your music

The buttons you need to use to listen to your favourite songs

The Alt button
The Alt button is the most important button to use when playing music. You'll need to keep this constantly held down when turning on tracks or selecting new ones

MORE MUSIC
So you've been listening to your favourite tunes, but you've just downloaded a new album that you'd like to add. Be sure to check out p138 and we'll show you how to include it for your own listening pleasure. Don't worry, it's really easy to do!

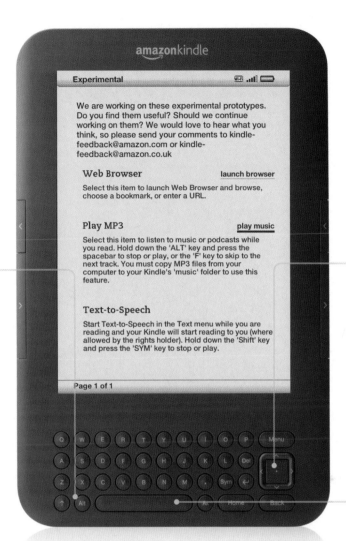

Experimental

We are working on these experimental prototypes. Do you find them useful? Should we continue working on them? We would love to hear what you think, so please send your comments to kindle-feedback@amazon.com or kindle-feedback@amazon.co.uk

Web Browser   launch browser

Select this item to launch Web Browser and browse, choose a bookmark, or enter a URL.

Play MP3   play music

Select this item to listen to music or podcasts while you read. Hold down the 'ALT' key and press the spacebar to stop or play, or the 'F' key to skip to the next track. You must copy MP3 files from your computer to your Kindle's 'music' folder to use this feature.

Text-to-Speech

Start Text-to-Speech in the Text menu while you are reading and your Kindle will start reading to you (where allowed by the rights holder). Hold down the 'Shift' key and press the 'SYM' key to stop or play.

Page 1 of 1

Quiet please
So you now have the ability to play music on your Kindle to add further enjoyment to your books, magazines and newspapers. Just remember that not everyone shares the same taste, so you might want to use your headphones!

Stopping/ starting music
It's easy to listen to your music. Simply scroll down to play music using your five-way controller and press the Enter button. You'll now hear your music playing

Skipping to the next track
You can turn music on and off by first holding down the Alt button and then pressing the spacebar. If you want to skip to the next track (you can't skip back) hold down the Alt button and press 'F'.

03: Navigate the menu

This is the Menu screen. This allows you to do all sorts of things, from turning your Wireless connection on and off to shopping in the Kindle Store or changing your settings. Use the five-way controller to select and press 'Experimental'.

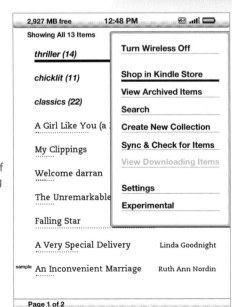

2,927 MB free   12:48 PM

Showing All 13 Items

thriller (14)

chicklit (11)

classics (22)

A Girl Like You (a

My Clippings

Welcome darran

The Unremarkable

Falling Star

A Very Special Delivery   Linda Goodnight

sample An Inconvenient Marriage   Ruth Ann Nordin

Page 1 of 2

Turn Wireless Off

Shop in Kindle Store

View Archived Items

Search

Create New Collection

Sync & Check for Items

View Downloading Items

Settings

Experimental

04: Play music

You are now on the Experimental screen. Ignore the Web Browser option and use the five-way controller to select and activate music. Voila! You can now hear your favourite tunes. Hold the Alt key and press the spacebar to stop and start tracks.

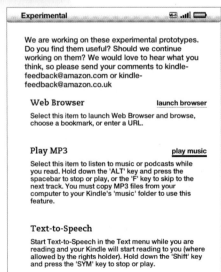

Experimental

We are working on these experimental prototypes. Do you find them useful? Should we continue working on them? We would love to hear what you think, so please send your comments to kindle-feedback@amazon.com or kindle-feedback@amazon.co.uk

Web Browser   launch browser

Select this item to launch Web Browser and browse, choose a bookmark, or enter a URL.

Play MP3   play music

Select this item to listen to music or podcasts while you read. Hold down the 'ALT' key and press the spacebar to stop or play, or the 'F' key to skip to the next track. You must copy MP3 files from your computer to your Kindle's 'music' folder to use this feature.

Text-to-Speech

Start Text-to-Speech in the Text menu while you are reading and your Kindle will start reading to you (where allowed by the rights holder). Hold down the 'Shift' key and press the 'SYM' key to stop or play.

Page 1 of 1

Get books from alternative sites

You can get eBooks from sites other than Amazon, and we show you how it's done…

The Kindle is a relatively open platform, which means that although content that you buy from Amazon itself is tied to your own user account, it's also possible to download other books and audio material to it from a variety of different sources. The easiest way to do this is to locate a site that legally provides free eBooks, and then download the books in the correct format, connect your Kindle to your computer and then drag and drop the files onto it so that they become available to read.

The great thing is that eBooks are very small in size, so you can load up hundreds if you like. Books that are free tend to be in the public domain, so you're not likely to find the latest bestsellers for free – it tends to be older works by authors who have long since passed away. Given the excellent quality of many of the books though, it's a great way to get loads of content for free, and legally. All you have to do is run a simple Google search along the lines of 'free legal eBooks' and you will be presented with loads of results. Follow the links and you can download the books to your Mac or PC, then copy them across and have hours of reading pleasure, all without spending any money! Explore the rich and varied world of free eBooks today.

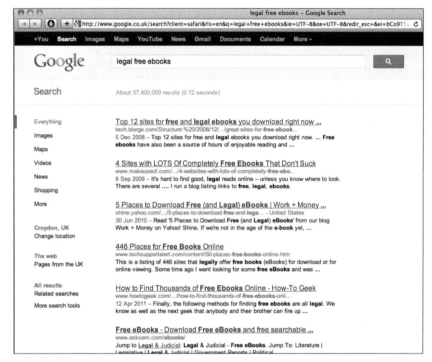

"Download the books, connect your Kindle to your computer and then drag and drop the files onto it"

01: Run a search

A simple Google search for 'free legal eBooks' (meaning legal to download, not books about the law) reveals hundreds of results. Follow a link or two: this site, for example, lists all of the top sources for free books.

02: Find a site

Here we have found a site called **manybooks.net** (as featured on p127) and it provides links to lots of free content. Search for a title or browse, then go to the Download box on the right and choose the mobipocket format and click Download.

Dropping books onto your Kindle

How to get third-party books onto your device

Capacity
Look at the capacity readout when your Kindle is connected to your computer to see how much space remains. EBooks take up very little space

Files
You can see a mixture of files, all readable by the Kindle. If a file appears here but doesn't show up on the Kindle's screen, it may not be in a readable format

Documents folder
Your Kindle stores its eBooks and other readable documents in the Documents folder, and it is here that you must drag and drop third-party content in order to be able to read it on the Kindle

Kindle drive
Connect your Kindle to your Mac or PC and it should appear as a drive. On Windows it will be in My Computer and on a Mac it appears on the Desktop and in the sidebar

KNOW THE FORMATS
The Kindle can read books in various different formats but there are quite a few out there, and not all will work. If in doubt, try to get .mobi-formatted books. If a book won't appear on your Kindle even after having been transferred, it's probably not in a compatible format

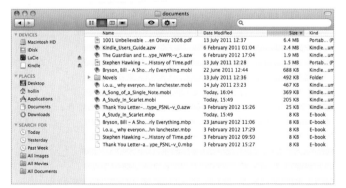

03: Drag the file

The file should download and you can click in your browser to reveal it. Connect your Kindle and then drag the file or files to the Documents folder inside the Kindle as it appears on your desktop. Files placed here will appear on your Home screen.

04: View on Kindle

Eject your Kindle from your computer and you should find that the book or books you dragged are now available to read. If they don't appear, check that the downloaded books were in the .mobi format and copied across into the correct folder.

Convert other formats to .mobi

The Kindle likes its eBooks in the .mobi format, but there are many other styles out there. We show you how to get other book types into the best format

Like with audio and video files, digital books come in a number of different formats. This is partly because they have been developed by different companies to work on competing devices, and partly because some formats have different features to others. The multitude of formats on offer can be a little confusing when you're browsing for books. Anything you buy from Amazon or on your Kindle will be in the right format of course, but other files that you download may not. It will be possible to drag and drop these devices onto your Kindle, but they may very well not show up in your list of books.

In recognition of this problem, a number of people have developed websites and applications that can convert from one format to another. In fact there's no real need to download an application and certainly not to spend any money, since all the tools you need to convert books into the Kindle's .mobi format are available for free and run in web browsers. You'll need an internet connection of course, but steer clear of any sites that ask you to register or pay for this service. It's available for free, and it's easy to use. So if you have downloaded or been sent an eBook in a format that isn't showing up on your Kindle, follow our helpful guide to format conversion and you'll be happily reading in no time.

"All the tools you need to convert books are available for free"

Choosing a book to convert
Converting eBooks to the Kindle's format is easy and free online

Choose the file
By clicking the Choose button in your browser you are confirming that the book selected in the file list above will be uploaded and prepared for conversion

Choose a book
A variety of formats exist but not all are readable by the Kindle. Here we can choose any format of book to upload for conversion

Format
In the Target eBook Reader menu you can choose between several models of Kindle and, on conversion, the website will process the files to suit your device

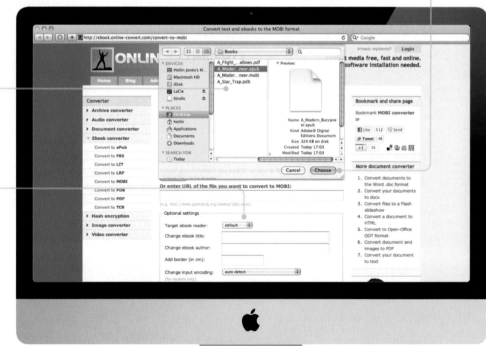

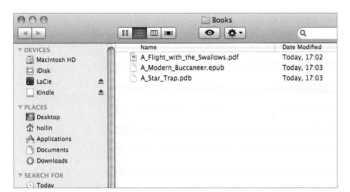

01: Prepare your books

You may see that, on your computer, the files show with no preview. If you double-click on them, you are told that there is no application available to open them with.

02: Google search

Find a website that will convert the files for you for free. There are applications for this but it's quicker, cleaner and easier to find a website that will do it. Run a Google search for 'convert to .mobi'.

03: Pick a site

Here we have chosen **ebook.online-convert.com**, though there are others that you can choose. This one has a nice interface and lets you choose your target eBook reader in a handy drop-down menu.

04: Choose a file

Click on the Choose File button on the website and then navigate to where your files are stored. It makes sense to create a folder so that you can keep track of everything more easily.

05: Upload the book

Highlight the file and click Choose. When the file chooser window closes, the book has uploaded to the site and then we can move on to choose what format we want to convert it to.

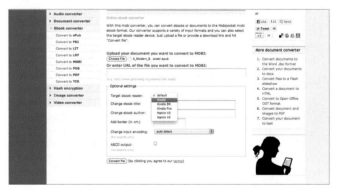

06: Choose a format

This website very helpfully provides an option to convert straight to a Kindle format, so choose Kindle from the Target eBook reader dropdown menu. Now click the Convert File button.

The next step

07: Wait for conversion

The conversion process might take a minute or two, especially if the book is very long. If it takes a while the site will give you the option to receive an email when the conversion is complete. Typically though it should not take more than a couple of minutes.

08: Get the file

Once the conversion has finished, the website will try to automatically download the file to your computer. Depending on what browser you are using, you may be prompted to save the file. On other systems it might be placed into your Downloads folder.

09: Locate the book

Locate the downloaded file on your system and you should find that it now has the .mobi suffix and may have gained an icon, meaning that the system knows what it is. Connect your Kindle and it should appear on your Desktop or, if you're on Windows, in My Computer.

10: Transfer the book

Drag and drop the newly converted book, along with any other books you want to transfer, onto the Kindle by putting them into the Documents folder inside the Kindle drive. They should take only a few seconds to copy over since the files are relatively small in size.

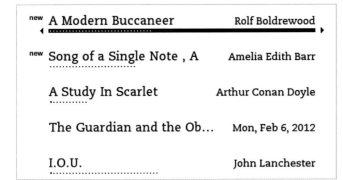

11: View on the Kindle

Eject your Kindle from your computer and go to the Home screen. There, you should see the newly converted book appear in your list since it is now in a format that the Kindle can read. If it doesn't appear, go back and check that the file copied to the device.

> particularly the privileged citizens of Sydney, I had always taken a leading part. More than once, in a hard-fought finish, had I been lifted out fainting or insensible.
>
> My curling fair hair and blue eyes bore token of our Norse blood and Anglo-Norman descent. The family held a tradition that our surname came from Taillefer, the warrior minstrel who rode in the forefront of Duke William's army at Hastings.

12: Read your book

Press the Enter button with the book selected on your Kindle and you should find it opens as normal. You should be able to read and search it just as easily as if it was a book you had bought straight from the Kindle Store.

An alternative website

The website 2epub.com is another great free resource for converting books online

Supported documents
This section helpfully tells you what input formats and what output formats are supported by the site. If in doubt, look at the file suffix of the file you're wanting to convert

Select files
Choose up to five files to upload to the website. These can be in any eBook format supported by the site, or Word documents or text files. A list of compatible input types is shown above the menu

File conversion
This area shows the progress of the conversion from one format to another. If you are unsure you can leave these fields set to Auto and the optimum settings will be used automatically

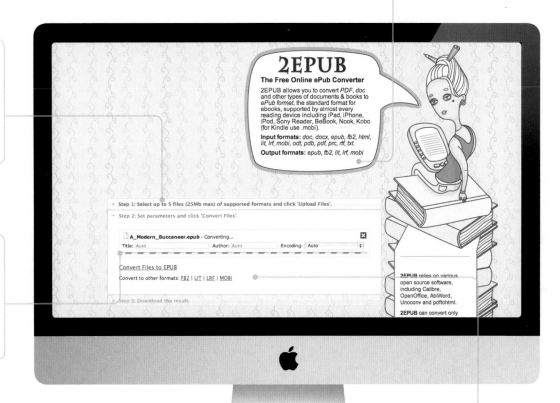

MAKE YOUR OWN EBOOKS
By uploading a Word or text file to an eBook conversion website and choosing to output it as a .mobi or other eBook format, you can turn any of your own documents into an eBook document that can be read on a Kindle

Choose a format
You can convert to a range of formats by simply clicking your preferred option here. For Kindles, click on the MOBI option and the site will set itself to convert your books to the correct Kindle format

Handy hints Some tips for converting eBooks

Name folders
It makes sense to keep files well organised and a good starting point is to keep them in a sensibly named folder on your hard drive so that you can find them.

Use .mobi files
Although Kindles can read other document types, it's best to stick to the .mobi format when converting as this offers maximum compatibility with the device.

Know your Kindle
Some sites let you specify a Kindle model when converting, so choose the correct one. Newer Kindles support colour, for example, but older ones do not.

Share documents
Use the online eBook conversion tools to convert your own Word, PDF and text documents into Kindle compatible formats and share them with your friends.

Back up
EBook files are small so it's no hassle and takes little time to back them up to a folder or an external hard drive, in case your Kindle ever gets lost or stolen.

Copy books to other devices

Transfer books from your Kindle to another mobile device and you get the benefit of being able to choose how you read

Content that you buy through the Kindle Store is linked to your Amazon account, but the Kindle also supports the dragging and dropping of eBooks and documents from other sources for reading as well. This means that the process works in reverse as well: you can copy books off your Kindle onto another device, provided the format is correct.

There are several reasons you might want to do this; for example, if someone wants to take the Kindle on holiday with them but you are halfway through reading a book and want to finish it. Or perhaps you are selling your Kindle and want to get the content off it and onto another e-reader. It's as simple as dragging and dropping the data from the Kindle's Documents folder when it is connected to your Mac or PC, and then using the equivalent process on the new device to copy the data onto that device. The Kindle's operating system makes it painless to transfer the files to your computer, or even in some cases directly onto another device. Here we guide you through the process.

"It's as simple as dragging and dropping the data from the Kindle's Documents folder"

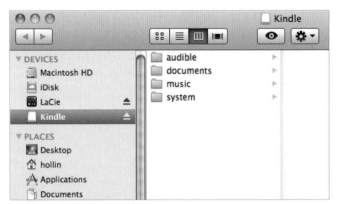

01: Connect the Kindle

Connect your Kindle to your Mac or PC using its USB cable and it should appear on the desktop if you are on a Mac, or in My Computer if you are using Windows. Double-click to open it.

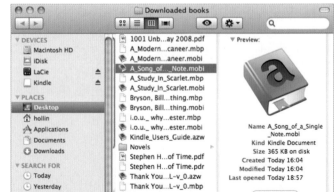

02: Select the books

Go into the Documents folder and select the books you would like to transfer. Create a folder on your desktop, then drag the books onto it. They will be duplicated and not removed from the Kindle.

Copying from the Kindle

How to get books off your Kindle

Disk space
You can monitor how much space is available on your Kindle by looking in the window that appears when it mounts on your computer

Document list
The books and other readable documents are stored here, and you can drag and drop them out of this list into another folder somewhere on your computer

The drive
Connect your Kindle to your Mac or PC and it will mount as a drive. On a Mac it will appear on the Desktop and on a PC it will appear in My Computer

Documents folder
The Kindle stores all its eBooks and PDF data inside the Documents folder so it's here you must look to find the data to copy

FILE CONVERSION
You may need to convert your .mobi files to another format before they can be read on your new device. This depends very much on what that device is. The good news is that there are some great free online file conversion tools available, see page 144.

03: Copy to a new device
The next step depends on what device you will be copying to. Here, we have an iPhone with the Kindle app installed so we can drag the books into the Sharing area in iTunes.

04: Read the books
Now on our iPhone we fire up the Kindle app and the books we transferred are there. Since we didn't delete the books on the Kindle, they remain available there too.

The next step

Use the Kindle app on iPad

Discover how you can access all of your purchased items for free through the free iPad and iPhone app and continue reading from where you left off

Purchasing and reading books from the Kindle Store isn't just limited to Kindle devices – you can access them on your smartphones and tablets too, such as iPhones, iPads and Androids.

Thanks to Amazon's Whispersync service, the books that you purchase and download to your Kindle device can also be accessed on the free Kindle apps for your other devices. Once you have downloaded the Kindle app and logged into your Amazon account, you will see an option called 'Archive (All Items)'.

Tap on this and you will be presented with a list of digital literature that you have previously purchased from the Kindle Store, and by tapping on an individual item you can instantly download it to the Home screen of your Kindle app at no extra cost – if you buy a book or other item for your Kindle, it can be accessed on all of your devices via the Kindle app.

What's more, Whispersync also logs and remembers where you are in a particular book, so that if you start reading one on your Kindle device, you can download it to, say, your iPad and continue reading from where you left off. It's a smooth, intuitive system that works brilliantly.

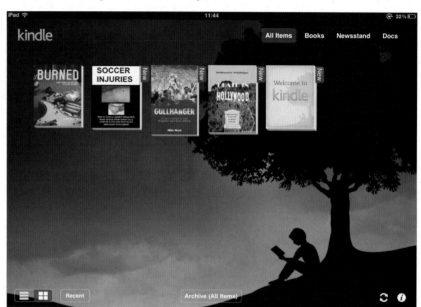

"If you buy a book on your Kindle, it can be accessed on all devices"

01: Log in

Download the Kindle app for free and then you will have to log in to your Amazon account to get started. Enter the same email address and password that you use to log in on your Kindle device and the choose the 'Register this Kindle' option.

02: Select Archive

Next, choose the 'Archive' option and all of the items that you have purchased and downloaded on your Kindle will appear on screen. Tap on an individual item to download it instantly to your Kindle app Home screen.

Access your Kindle content

Learn how to use Amazon's Whispersync service to continue reading on iPad…

Your items

Items that you tap on and download from the 'Archived Items' section will appear on the Home screen of your Kindle app. Now simply tap on a cover to open that particular item

Archived items

All of the items you have previously downloaded from the Kindle Store will be listed and be accessible from the 'Archived Items' section of the app. Tap on it to access them

Personal documents

If you would like to store and read personal documents through your Kindle app (it beats printing them), then you will be provided with an email address to send them to

Continue reading

If you have started reading a book on your Kindle device then Amazon's Whispersync technology means that you'll be able to pick up exactly where you left off. Just tap on the book and it will jump straight to the page you were on

GET MORE BOOKS

You can get more books to read through the Kindle app by either accessing the Amazon website directly from your smartphone or tablet's web browser or by downloading the free Amazon Windowshop app. The latter works best on iPhones and iPads as a welcoming interface and allows you to shop easily with confidence and browse the extensive range of digital publications available.

03: Access your items

Once all of your previously downloaded items have been downloaded from the archive (via Amazon's Whispersync system), they will be visible on your Kindle app Home screen when you tap on the 'Home' button at the bottom of the screen.

04: Continue reading

Thanks to Amazon's Whispersync system, when you tap on a book that you started reading on your Kindle device, it will open at the exact page that you got to. If you then read a few pages through the Kindle app, you'll be able to continue from your Kindle later too.

Use the Kindle app on Android

The free Kindle app for Android enables you to access all of your purchased content and grab more on the move

The beauty of Kindle is that it is an entity that is completely universal across all digital platforms beyond your Kindle device itself – including desktop computers, Apple iOS devices and Android.

With smartphones now supporting larger amounts of storage – much more than Kindle devices – you can store thousands of books and keep them organised within the Kindle app. Because the app is associated with an Amazon account, if you ever decide to switch phones (or you have multiple smartphones), you can take all your books with you. Then there's the 24/7 access to thousands of books wherever you are, provided you have data access.

There are a couple of downsides to the Kindle app, though. Firstly, it is highly dependent on the battery life of your device, and secondly the size of the screen isn't great. If your smartphone is small then the experience may be slightly less intuitive, but this isn't a major problem with a number of modern Android phones, like the Samsung Galaxy II S, whose 4.3-inch screen makes it far more ideal.

Like with the iPhone and iPad Kindle apps, the Android version is free and, once installed, you can access all of your previously purchased books and items so that you can have them with you at all times. And thanks to Amazon's Whispernet service, you will be able to continue reading where you left off – perfect!

"Access all of your previously purchased items on your Android"

Kindle interface
Getting to grips with how the Kindle app works

Your books
When you get more books they will start to populate the screen; you can switch to a Grid mode to view the books across the page

TRANSFERRING
Once you have registered your account with an Android device you can easily transfer over to another device. However it's best to remove the association before you sell your device or change contracts. To do this, head to the settings option and choose 'Deregister this device'.

Archived Items
This option lets you download previously purchased items to your Android Kindle app, so you have all of your books with you at all times

Kindle Store
You can access the Kindle Store through the app to purchase new books to add to your collection and then sync them across all devices

Manual Syncing
You can hit the 'Sync' button to instantly sync your items and the pages you have read to across all of your Kindle devices

01: Download

Ensure you either have a data or Wi-Fi connection. Launch the Market app and search for Kindle. Download the app and then it will automatically install. Once installed, launch the app and the option to read your previously purchased books through your Android phone is but a few moments away.

02: Register or log in

If you already have an Amazon account, which you will do if you have been using a Kindle device, simply type in your email address and password then click on 'Register'. Otherwise, you'll need to set up a new account, which you can also do through the app.

03: Sort By

Once into your account, go to the 'Archived Items' section and you'll be able to download previous purchases to the Android App. Press the 'Menu' button and choose 'Sort By', as this will sort your books into order using Title, Author or Most Recent, making it much easier to view your reading material.

04: View by List or Grid

The default view is List mode, but you may wish to view your books in a Grid formation so that you can really appreciate the fine detail on the digital covers as they are displayed. Press the Menu button and select 'More', then select the 'View' option and choose 'Grid' to change the arrangement.

05: Search items

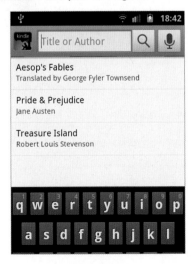

If you have hundreds of books downloaded to your Kindle Android app and want to find one quickly, press the Menu button and choose 'More'. Select the 'Search' option and then type in keywords that relate to the title or author of the book. The app will then provide a list of possibilities.

06: Kindle Store

You can access the Kindle Store by pressing the Menu button then choosing the 'Kindle Store' option. Here you can view the extensive range of digital literature and download items straight to your Android Kindle app. Press Back to return to the main interface when you have finished.

Read a Kindle book on your PC

It's just as easy to read Kindle books on your PC as it is on the Kindle itself! Learn how with our quick and easy guide

One of the best things about the Kindle is its portability, and it also has excellent battery life that makes it the perfect travelling companion. But, sometimes, you might want to also access the books you have bought or downloaded from your PC. Even though the Kindle works beautifully as a wireless device and can be used without a computer, it's nonetheless true that almost everyone has a computer these days. So the good news is that it's possible to download the Kindle for PC software from Amazon's website, enter your login details and then read the same books that you have on your Kindle on your PC, either by syncing the two devices or, more likely, by just letting the PC application download the books from your Amazon account.

There are a number of advantages to being able to read your books on your PC. The most obvious perhaps is the much larger screen sizes that home computers afford, and also the fact that they are in colour. This is less important for the pages of course, but it's nice to see the book covers as they were originally intended. The larger screen gives you more flexibility with the layout and also being able to interact with the text using the mouse means looking up definitions is a breeze too.

"The larger screen gives you more flexibility with the layout"

Managing Kindle for PC

Getting to know Kindle for PC's interface

Your library
This displays how many items are in your library and lets you see which have been downloaded and which archived. Click the circle icon to sync books with your account

Books
By viewing on your PC you can see covers in colour. Double-click to open a book or right-click to see more advanced reading options

Search
Search the Kindle Store directly from the app itself. Any books you buy will be automatically added to your account

Collections
Collections that you have created on your Kindle will be synced wirelessly to your Amazon account and will also be updated here in the app

FULL SCREEN
There's an option at the top of the screen in the View menu that enables you to switch Kindle for PC into Full Screen mode. This is perfect for getting rid of visual distractions and making it feel like you are reading a real book

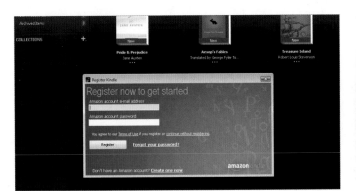

01: Download the software

Go to Amazon's website and download the Kindle for PC software. Install it following the instructions and then sign in to your account.

02: Go to your library

After signing in, you should see the books in your Amazon account appear in the software Click the Library button to see a list of them.

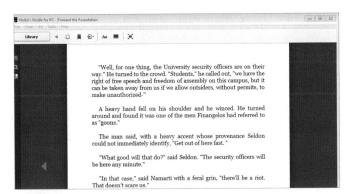

03: Read a book

Select a book and then double-click on it to open it at the start. You can also right-click on it to go to a specific page or the last page read.

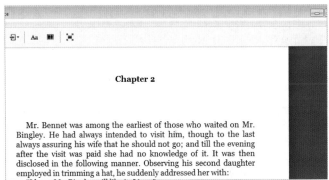

04: Change the view

Go to the buttons on the toolbar and click the Columns button. Here you can switch between single or multiple column view.

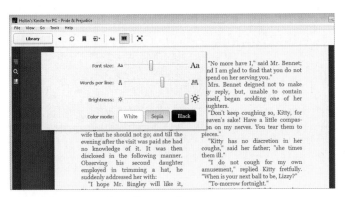

05: Change the font size

Click on the font icon and you can change the size of the font as well as the word spacing per line and even the background colour.

06: Define a word

Right-click on any word and the application will search for a suitable definition and display it for you if it is available.

Read a Kindle book on a Mac

Books that you buy or download onto your Kindle can also be read on your Mac, which is great news for when you're at your desk

The Kindle works really well as a standalone device, with Wi-Fi and 3G connectivity letting you use it independently of a computer. You don't need to own a computer to have a Kindle, but most people do anyway.

The good news is that your Mac and Kindle can play nicely together. If you go to Amazon's website and follow the links, you will be able to download the Kindle for Mac software. Double-click on the downloaded file to install it, and enter your Amazon login details so that

it can sync your books between your account and the Kindle for Mac application.

Reading on your Mac does, of course, have some advantages. For a start, the screen is larger. It also supports colour, and though the pages themselves are in black and white, the covers are usually in colour, which looks nice.

The Mac application also has more features than the Kindle simply by virtue of running on a computer. It's easier to interact with the text, add notes and other annotations and to quickly select chapters. Moreover, remember that the books you buy can be used on your Kindle and your Mac at the same time.

"The books you buy can be used on your Kindle and Mac at the same time"

Reading on your Mac

Exploring Kindle for Mac's interface

View options
It's easy to change the column view style, the size of the text and even the word spacing to suit your preferred style of reading

The text
Text can be easily selected with the mouse, and dictionary definitions called up. You can also make notes and highlight sections of the text

Library
Click the 'Library' button at any time to be taken back to your main library. Collections and other content will be synced via your Amazon account

Contents
Viewing on a computer makes it easier to see the list of contents and click on any chapter title to jump straight to it

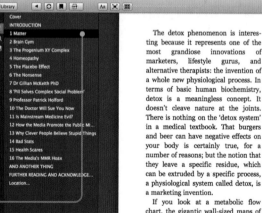

FULL SCREEN
There's an option in Kindle for Mac's menu that lets you view it in full-screen mode. This blocks out every other screen element and really makes it feel like you are reading a real book on your Mac.

01: Download the software

Go to Amazon.com and download the Kindle for Mac software. After installation, start it up and enter your Amazon login details.

02: Go to your library

Your books download automatically from your Amazon account. You can also connect via USB and sync it to transfer other items.

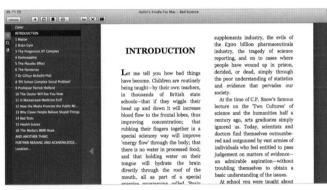

03: Open a book

Double-click on a book to open it. Click on the 'Contents' icon on the left to reveal the list of contents. Click on a chapter to jump to it.

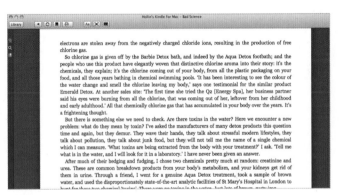

04: Switch view

Go to the toolbar at the top and click on the page icon. This switches between column and page view. Choose your favourite view type.

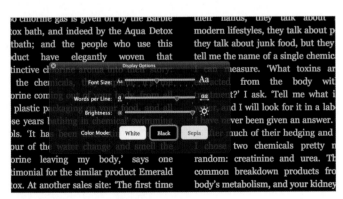

05: Change display

Click on the 'Display Options' button, and you can change font size, words per line and even reverse the colours.

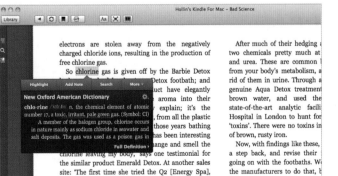

06: Look up a word

Right-click your mouse on any word in the text, and if it is available a dictionary definition will be displayed in a small pop-up window.

Helpdesk

Helpdesk

So you've got to grips with your Kindle but you may still have a few queries – here we tackle the most frequently asked questions

Emails

How do I check my email using my Kindle device?

You can check your email on the Kindle with the experimental built-in web browser. For Hotmail, Yahoo Mail and AOL webmail services, this is just like you would use it as if it were a desktop browser; you log in with your email and password. For the Wi-Fi model you need to be connected to your home wireless router or a hotspot. It's also possible to get email from services that use Microsoft Outlook, though your email provider needs to have enabled webmail as well.

Many ISPs that deliver your mail through Outlook will have a webmail service so that you can access your mail while away from the home. Again, you'll need your email address and password but also the web address of the webmail client for this. Any mail you download and read here will still remain on the server for download when you get back home.

"You can check your email on the Kindle using the built-in web browser"

Step-by-step | Log in and check email

1: Launch the browser

Press the Home button then the Menu button. Navigate down to 'Experimental'. Select this to bring up the entry for the Web Browser. Highlight 'Launch Browser' and press 'Confirm'.

2: Go to the website

The first list is of bookmarks. Navigate down to the bottom and select 'Close Bookmarks'. Use the keyboard to enter the web address of your email supplier. Select 'Done' and then 'Go To'.

3: Enter details

Use the zoom control to find the icon for email and then press 'Confirm'. Now you need to use the cursor to select 'Mail'. Finally, use the cursor to select and then enter your email address and password.

Battery life
How can I stop the battery from running down so quickly?

The great thing about the Kindle is that you can load it with books and take it on holiday with you and never have to worry about charging it up while away. In fact, with Wi-Fi and 3G turned off, Amazon claims that the Kindle will last a month from regular use between charges. The Kindle uses power when it refreshes screens or renders text. Once it has done that, it doesn't use any power – that's why the Sleep mode which uses the screensavers is as power efficient as turning the Kindle off completely. However, if you find that your battery power isn't lasting very long, there are usually two causes. One is that the battery hasn't been fully charged in the first place and the other is that it is constantly using the radio signal for Wi-Fi and 3G. It can also be the sign of a faulty battery, which entails returning the device to Amazon.

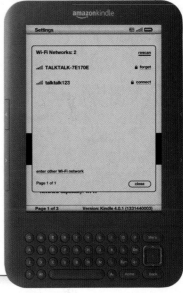

■ *Constant scanning for Wi-Fi networks is a battery drain, so turn Wi-Fi off when it's not required*

Step-by-step | Turning the Wi-Fi signal off

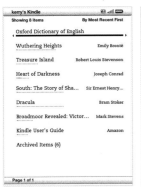

1: Go into Settings
One way to save battery power when you don't need a constant Wi-Fi signal is to turn the latter off. To start, press the Home button.

2: Turn Wi-Fi off
Press the Menu button and navigate up to 'Turn Wireless Off'. Select this and it will immediately be turned off. The signal strength and Wi-Fi icons will disappear.

3: Turn back on
When you next need to access archived books or the Store, press Menu then select the 'Turn Wireless On' option. It will connect a few seconds later.

Screen grab

How do I take a screenshot on the Kindle?

There's often a time when you think, 'Ah, I just need to remind myself of that,' or want to pass something on to a friend. It could be a list of new books featured on Amazon, a poetic turn of verse or a review of your own eBook. Well, one of the hidden features of the Kindle is the ability to take screen grabs. Note that the process is different for the Kindle Keyboard and the Kindle 4, which has a virtual keyboard.

On the Kindle Keyboard model, you need to press Alt+Shift+G on the keyboard to take a grab of what's currently on the screen. On the Kindle 4 you need to press the Keyboard and the Menu button at the same time. This is a lot more hit and miss, especially if you're already looking at a menu. The screen grabs are placed in the same folder on your Kindle as your eBooks and are in the .gif format. You can find them in the Documents folder.

Step-by-step | Screen-grab new book releases

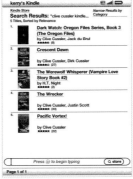

1: Go to the site
Press the Home button then the Menu button. Navigate down to 'Shop in Kindle Store' and select it. Navigate down to the search engine line to search for a specific author.

2: Find the author
As you type, a list of suggestions starts to appear. Close the keyboard and navigate up to select the best match. Here we are selecting Clive Cussler books that are new on Kindle.

3: Take the grab
The search results show a list of new books. Time to take the screen grab. Kindle Keyboard owners press Alt+Shift+G; Kindle 4 owners press Keyboard and Menu simultaneously.

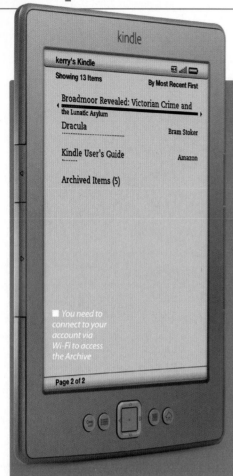

Weak Wi-Fi

What can you do when you can't connect to a home Wi-Fi signal?

We can start by assuming that your Wi-Fi router at home works properly and that you have entered the security code into the Kindle to access it. However, you can't connect and don't know why. The first reason could be that you entered the router password wrongly. Remember, this

"If the router isn't connected, your Kindle won't be"

isn't your Kindle or computer password, it's one on the router itself. The next question is to work out how many devices are connected to the router at once. There is normally a limit on connections; check you aren't exceeding it, causing your

Kindle connection to fail. Next, go have a look at the modem/router itself and see that the lights for connection to the internet and wireless are on. If the router isn't connected, your Kindle won't be. If you only have a B or G-class router, the signal may not be strong enough; it could be being blocked or interfered with.

Also ensure that your Kindle is close enough to be able to connect – check the signal strength icons on your Kindle itself. If you only have one bar of signal strength, it's quite weak. Move closer and consider upgrading to a more powerful router. Does your router have MAC filtering enabled? If so, the Kindle won't be able to connect until you add the Kindle's MAC address to the router's list of acceptable addresses.

Step-by-step | Checking for available Wi-Fi networks

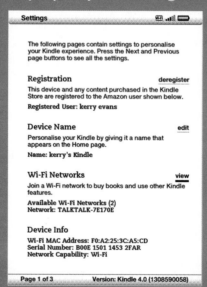

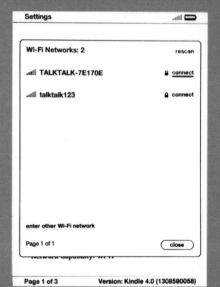

1: Turn Wi-Fi on
Firstly, press the Home button and then the Menu button. The topmost entry on the screen should say 'Turn Wireless Off'. If it says 'Turn Wireless On' then it isn't currently active. Navigate to the entry and press 'Confirm'.

2: Check the networks
The Wi-Fi receiver will now be active and can detect networks. Press the Menu button again to bring it back up. Navigate down to 'Settings' and press 'Confirm'. Navigate down to 'Wi-Fi Networks', highlight 'View' and press 'Confirm'.

3: Select the network
There will now be a list of the available networks that the Kindle can see. Navigate down to the one you want to connect to. Press 'Confirm' to connect to it. You should then enter your router password once more.

Kindle Store

Why can't I connect to the Kindle Store?

There is a curious issue where you can connect your Kindle to the internet (ie the web browsing works) but you can't connect to the Kindle Store. The device simply reports an 'unable to connect' error. It's usually because of an error on your Kindle itself, but there's another cause that's harder to track down. This issue can be caused by using a firewall on your router and this can block certain types of access, creating the problem. Try temporarily turning off the router firewall to see what effect that has.

Also, another cause is that of router security protocols. Many people have reported problems when they have been using WPA2 security. Although the Kindle supports this, if you change the router so that it is using WPA only, then there's a good chance it will now work. If it isn't any of these things then there's one trick left to try which, thankfully, is easy to do…

Step-by-step | Quick fix for Store error

1: Go into settings
The quick fix involves restarting your Kindle. Firstly, press the Home button and then the Menu button. Navigate down the list to Settings.

2: Restart the Kindle
Press Confirm to access Settings and then navigate down to Restart. Select this and then press Confirm to action it. There will be a pause for a few seconds.

3: Connect to Store
The Kindle will flash and show the booting-up sequence. Press the Menu button and you should be able to select 'Shop in Kindle Store' and access it.

Lost Kindle

What do I do if I lose my Kindle?

If your Kindle is lost or gets stolen, the immediate problem is that any gift or certificate cards registered to your account can be used by a thief with the 1-Click buying system, and unfortunately gift cards are not refunded if your Kindle is stolen. You do have some protection for any credit or debit cards that are linked to the account, but it's relatively easy for a thief to rapidly run up high amounts of charges. Also, a thief with your Kindle can potentially access your email account or other websites that you've logged in to.

There are two things you should do if the worst happens. Firstly, deregister the Kindle so it isn't linked to your account. Second, get in touch with Amazon's customer services and report it lost. They will blacklist it so it can't be used to access the Whispernet service.

> "A thief with your Kindle can access your email account or websites you've logged in to"

Step-by-step | What to do if your Kindle is stolen

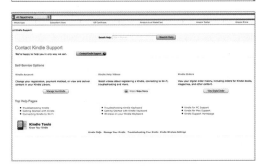

1: Go to Amazon
Go to the Amazon website and log in as usual. Click on 'Your Account' and then on 'Manage Your Kindle'.

2: Remove the device
Click on 'Manage Your Devices' on the left to bring up the full list of Kindle devices and apps registered. Simply click on 'Deregister' for the Kindle hardware.

3: Contact customer services
From there, go to 'Kindle Help Home' on the left-hand side. Now, again of the left-hand side of the screen, go to 'Contact Kindle Support' and follow the instructions.

Password

What can I do if I lose my password?

It might be that you've never even thought about putting a password on your Kindle, but there are good reasons for doing so. One is that if the Kindle is lost, borrowed or accessed by your kids, with the 1-Click purchasing system, anyone can run up a large bill before you know about it. The other is that with access to your device someone could equally just mess around with it, change your collections, delete

books, and post comments and highlights that you don't agree with. However, make sure the password is something you can remember easily because if you forget it you will have to reset the Kindle, which will remove all the content on it. You will then

have to register your Kindle again on the Amazon website to link the content to it. This will then display all the content that has been purchased for your Kindle and you will be able to download everything to the device again.

■ *If you forget your password, you'll have to re-register*

Step-by-step | How to set and reset

1: Set the password
To set a password in the first place, press the Home button then Menu. Navigate to 'Settings' and select it. Move onto the second page.

2: Turn it on
Navigate to 'Device Password' and select it. You can enter your password, re-enter it to confirm it and also use a password hint to make it easy to remember.

3: Reset the Kindle
When you switch on the Kindle, you must enter the password. If you've lost it, enter 'resetmykindle' as the password and press 'OK'. The device will then reset.

Sync

What can I do to make sure annotations sync across devices?

One of the options on the Kindle is to synchronise the last page read, collections and notes/highlights/annotations across all the devices registered to your Amazon account. It does this by making an automatic backup using the Wi-Fi signal for Whispersync. One reason for it not working is if some of your devices are not in Wi-Fi zones when a new annotation has been made on a different device. You can turn this feature off as well, which can be useful if you are lending one Kindle-based device to a family member while you use another one. To make notes and highlights when reading, just press the keyboard to move the cursor into position. Press 'Confirm' then select which kind of annotation you want to use. Create the note or highlight and save it. It will then appear in the text every time you look at it. With Whispersync it will also propagate across all your devices.

Step-by-step | Make a highlight across devices

1: Create the highlight
The first step is to actually create the highlight in the text. Open an eBook and go to the place you want it. Create the highlighted section and then save it.

2: Tune the Settings
Press the Home button then Menu. Navigate down to 'Settings' and select it. Go to the third page of Settings and move down to 'Annotations Backup'. This should be set to on.

3: Manually sync across
This should work automatically. Or press Home then Menu and navigate to 'Sync & Check for Items'; select it to manually force a sync across devices.

Reset

How do I perform a reset and why is it necessary?

There are times when the Kindle can decide that it's had enough. This can present itself as a frozen, unresponsive screen, the physical keyboard of the Kindle 3 or the virtual one of the Kindle 4 not operating, or the back and forward keys not doing anything. In these cases the software that runs the Kindle has crashed and it needs to be restarted. The simplest way of doing this is to press the power button and hold onto it until the screen goes blank, then release the button. The LED light blinks three times after five seconds and the screen blanks out after around ten. Release the button. The Kindle has been powered down. Turn it back on again

and it will probably be okay. If it isn't, repeat the process but this time hold the power button down even after it goes blank for around 20 seconds. This performs a hard reset and should do the trick. If the Kindle comes on but doesn't work properly, it can be because of additional components that have been installed. In this case you need to reset it back to the Factory Defaults. This is the state it was shipped in and is completely empty and clean. Before you do this, archive all the books you want to keep first. You will have to register again with the same name to be able to retrieve all your books from Amazon that you've previously paid for or archived.

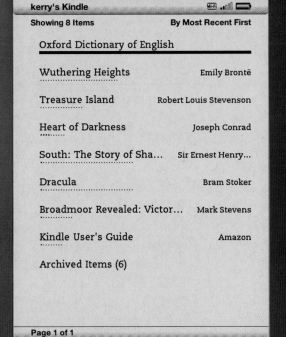

1: Into the Settings

Press the Home button and then Menu. Navigate down to 'Settings' and press 'Confirm'. In the menu that comes up, press the Menu button again. Navigate down to 'Reset to Factory Defaults' and then press 'Confirm'.

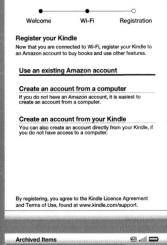

2: Accept the warning

At the scary notice, select 'OK'. You will then get the start-up message as it reboots. Select your language then enter your Wi-Fi network details and password. Once connected, select 'Close' to progress.

3: Configure the Kindle

Now select 'Use an existing Amazon account' and enter your email address and password. Press the Home button and select the 'Archive'. Simply navigate to each book and press 'Confirm' to download. Repeat for all books.

Helpdesk

The problem with eBooks

When things go wrong with your eBooks, this is where you need to come to sort them out

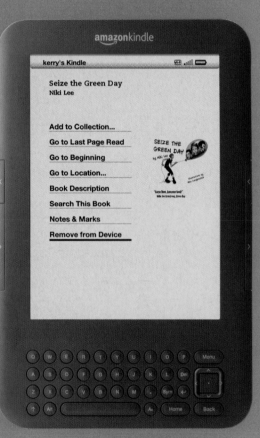

■ *Removing a book from your Kindle is easy; just select the 'Remove from Device' option*

"If an eBook won't open, it means it didn't download properly… Delete it, restart the device, then download it again"

TIP 1

Removing books you've read

To remove a book, press the Home button to get a listing of them. Navigate to the one in question, then press right on the control pad. Scroll down to 'Remove from Device' and press the 'Confirm' button on it. It will ask if you want to continue. Ensure 'OK' is selected and press 'Confirm'.

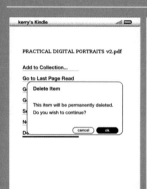

in which they pursued their trade, and, while confirming earlier information as to the extreme severity of the ice conditions in this sector of the Antarctic, they were able to give advice that was worth attention.

It will be convenient to state here briefly some of the considerations that weighed with me at that time and in the weeks that followed. I knew that the ice had come far north that season and, after listening to the suggestions of the whaling

TIP 2

An eBook refuses to open

If you want to read an eBook and it won't open, it's possible that it didn't download properly. Delete the eBook as in Tip 1, press the Home button and then the Menu button. Navigate to 'Settings' then press the Menu button again. From the new options, select 'Restart' then download the book again.

TIP 3

Personal document notes not syncing

Files transferred by USB and unconverted PDFs don't support syncing across devices. Otherwise press the Home button, then Menu. Navigate to 'Sync & Check for Items'. Press 'Confirm'. Repeat the process on any other Kindle device that you want to sync the doc and notes to.

TIP 4

Not restoring last page read

If you go back to an eBook and it doesn't automatically restore the page you were on, it's because the Kindle was turned off before it could save it. Go to the Home screen before powering the Kindle down and instead of turning the Kindle off, put it into Sleep mode.

USB Drive Mode

If you want to read or shop on your Kindle while continuing to charge over USB, please keep the USB cable attached, but eject your Kindle from your computer.

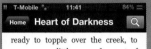

ready to topple over the creek, to sweep every little man of us out of his little existence. And it moved not. A deadened burst of mighty splashes and snorts reached us from afar, as though an icthyosaurus had been taking a bath of glitter in the great river. 'After all,' said the boiler-maker in a reasonable tone, 'why shouldn't we get the rivets?' Why not, indeed! I did not know of any reason why we shouldn't. 'They'll come in three weeks,' I said

TIP 5
Kindle not recognised over USB

If your computer doesn't recognise the Kindle when connected via USB, you can't transfer eBooks. Try plugging the USB lead into a different USB port on the PC and then try restarting your PC with the Kindle connected. Finally, restart your Kindle as per Tip 2.

TIP 6
Skipping pages when turning on

This usually occurs because there are multiple Kindles – or readers on other devices – that are accessing the same eBook. The last page read is synced across all devices. Check that no one else is reading the same book on one of your devices.

TIP 7
Transferred file format not recognised

If you can't read a file, it's because the Kindle doesn't recognise the file format. The most common examples are password-protected PDFs and EPUB-format eBooks. Convert the file to a suitable format and transfer it again.

■ *You need to ensure that transferred files are in a supported file format*

> "If you can't read a file, it's because the Kindle doesn't recognise the format"

■ *Photos need to be in the correct file format – and not too large – to be displayed properly*

TIP 8
Photos don't display in eBook

If you copy a document to the Kindle yourself and you find that some of the photos are not displayed, it's either because they are in an unsupported format or that they are too large. Try reformatting your document with JPEG images, rather than TIFFs, and keep the file size for them at under 128K.

TIP 9
PDF looks too small

Having copied a PDF file to your Kindle, the text and pictures can appear too small. This usually happens when the PDF pages are landscape orientation. Try pressing the Menu button, navigate to 'Zoom & Contrast' and either select a larger scaling size or use 'Screen Rotation' in landscape mode.

TIP 10
Can't read the text clearly

If the text of a document or book appears too thin or weak so that it's difficult to read, press the Menu button. Navigate down, select the 'Zoom & Contrast' option and move the cursor to 'Contrast'. Move it again onto 'Darker' or 'Darkest' for much more contrast.

Helpdesk

Upgrade

Why should I and how do I upgrade the Kindle firmware?

There are times when crashes and lock-ups are caused by how the software that runs the Kindle works. When Amazon tracks down the bugs, it issues a firmware update. Previously this has been rolled out automatically over a Wi-Fi connection, but minor upgrades tend not to be. The other reason for wanting firmware upgrades is that they often include extra functionality or bundled apps.

The way to find out the latest firmware for your Kindle model is to go to the Amazon website and click on the 'Help' button in the top-right corner. In the panel of Help topics on the left, click on 'Kindle'. Look down this list for 'Kindle Software Updates' and click on that. Now select your Kindle from those shown. This will show the latest version of the Kindle firmware. If it's newer than the one on your Kindle, then you should consider updating it. You don't have to unless it's a major update that adds a feature that your Kindle will struggle without.

To check what version of the firmware your Kindle is using, press the Home button first. Then press the Menu button and navigate to the entry for 'Settings'. Select this and at the bottom of the display you will see the current firmware version for your Kindle.

> ## "When Amazon tracks down the bugs, it issues a firmware update"

■ To find the latest firmware for your Kindle, go to the Amazon website

Step-by-step | Updating the Kindle firmware manually

1: Download file

The first step is to go to the page on the Amazon website where the latest firmware is detailed. It also contains a download link. Click on this and note where you are saving it to on your computer.

2: Connect the Kindle

Turn your Kindle on and plug it into your computer. When the dialog box opens showing the files on your Kindle, drag the update file from wherever you saved it, into the main folder.

3: Update and reboot

When done, disconnect the Kindle. Press Home and then Menu. Navigate down the list to 'Settings' and press 'Confirm'. Now press Menu again and select 'Update your Kindle'. Select 'OK' to update.

Rotate screen

Why doesn't my Kindle automatically rotate the screen?

If you have used the Kindle 3 Keyboard model and noticed that it automatically rotates the screen when you turn it from portrait to landscape, and vice versa, you may be surprised when it doesn't work on the Kindle 4. One of the many features removed, to reduce costs, is the gyro sensor that detects when the Kindle has been rotated. As such, it doesn't have the facility to automatically rotate. If you have a Kindle Keyboard and it isn't rotating the screen, it might be that it is turned off. Press the Text key and check to see if it rotates then. If it doesn't, go into the Settings and make sure the 'Auto rotate' option is selected. Also, check how much battery power is left. Very low battery status can disable rotation. The final option is to restart the Kindle, which can fix the problem.

■ *If the screen doesn't auto-rotate, it could be down to the settings or low battery power*

Step-by-step | Rotating screens on Kindle 4

1: Load a file
Normal A5-format books don't need to be rotated, but something like a PDF may be the wrong aspect ratio for portrait viewing. Press Menu then select 'Zoom & Contrast'.

2: Change the rotation
Navigate down to the 'Screen Rotation' section and manually select a landscape orientation. Confirm this and the page will rotate. It may not fit, so tinker with the zoom settings.

3: If all else fails
If screen rotation doesn't work on either model of the Kindle, press the Home button and then Menu. Select 'Settings' and navigate down to 'Restart'. Select this.

Wi-Fi Network

How do I join new Wi-Fi networks?

When out travelling, you may well have your Kindle with you. Trouble is that even if you have a 3G model, the coverage isn't anything like consistent or universal. For Wi-Fi models the problem is worse because you have to find a free Wi-Fi hotspot. The Kindle can detect any broadcasting Wi-Fi hotspot and let you enter a password for it. It will then remember this network and connect automatically the next time it sees it. This works fine for hotspots in pubs and hotels, but for cafes and places like McDonald's where the Wi-Fi is provided by a third-party service, The Cloud, you may need to register as well. Once you have achieved a connection to the Wi-Fi signal, you will need to launch the experimental browser and in the case of The Cloud, register your email address and a password. Only then will it let you onto the network.

Step-by-step | Connecting to a Wi-Fi network

1: Find a service
When travelling, your home network won't be available so you need to look for a hotspot where you are. Press the Home button and then Menu. Navigate down to 'Settings'.

2: Go to network
Navigate down to 'Wi-Fi Networks' and select 'View'. This will show all networks visible. If the one you want is not there, select 'Rescan'. Now select the network you want to use.

3: Enter the password
The hotspot owner will have provided a password, so enter it now to connect. For some services, you may need to register using the web browser.

Helpdesk

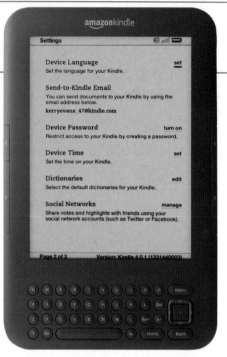

Dictionary

My Kindle is using the wrong dictionary – how do I change it?

One of the impressive things about the Kindle is that it can display the interface in German, English, US English, Spanish, French, Italian and Portuguese. It can also use dictionaries from any of those languages independently of whether the main interface is using it. This can be useful when learning a foreign language, or if reading a text and needing to know the American spelling. You may look on your Kindle and not find any alternative dictionaries. That's because they are all in the Archive. Navigate to the 'Archive' section and download them from there. Once they are on your device, they can be used by it. The problem can come if you notice that you're reading a book and it's being flagged for incorrect spellings. Usually this is because the US dictionary has been loaded and you want the Queen's English, or vice versa.

1: Set the language

To change the language used by the Kindle, press the Home button and then Menu. Navigate down to 'Settings' and select it. Press the Next Page button once.

Step-by-step | Changing the language and dictionary

2: Select language

Select the first entry to set the Device Language. Navigate and select the one you want to use. The device will then use this for the interface – it won't translate eBooks.

3: Change dictionary

On the same screen as Device Language is an option for 'Dictionaries'. Select this, then navigate to the one you want to use. Select to apply it when reading eBooks.

"The Kindle device can also use dictionaries from any of the supported languages"

Ghosting

My Kindle has ghosting on the screen – how can I get rid of it?

There are two issues here that seem similar but, in fact, are poles apart. The first is that if you get graphical glitches and lines on the screen that don't come up, you need to restart your Kindle. If that doesn't clear the problem, it's a major fault with the E-Ink system and you need to contact Amazon customer services to organise returning your device. The other issue is that of actual ghosting on the screen where there are traces of the previous page as you turn to a new one. On Kindle 3 devices and earlier, the screen was refreshed every time the page was turned on an eBook. This actually uses more power as the E-Ink only consumes power when a new screen is being rendered or refreshed. On the Kindle 4, Amazon changed the system so that the refreshes only happen every five pages. It can mean there's a ghost impression until that fifth page refresh.

Step-by-step | Get rid of the ghosting

1: Firmware update

Amazon has recently acknowledged this problem and introduced a firmware update to fix it by enabling you to refresh your Kindle 4 screen after every page. Press the Home button.

2: Go into Settings

Press the Menu button and then go into the 'Settings'. At the bottom of the page is the firmware version number. If it is not 4.0.1 then you will need to download and update the Kindle first.

3: Set refresh rate

Press the 'next page' button twice and navigate down to 'Page Refresh'. This is only present on 4.0.1. Select this to make every page refresh, which will clear up the ghosting.

■ *You can manage your Kindle hardware and account from the Amazon website*

Manage

How can I manage my Kindle account?

While the Kindle itself offers a one-stop method of buying books and magazines and being able to store them directly on the device, if anything goes wrong with it, you will need access to the backups. Also, any personal documents that you sent to the Kindle with the Amazon email service will disappear as well.

Fortunately, they are also stored on the Amazon server and can be retrieved if you don't have the originals any more. You have 5GB of storage space for personal documents so it's unlikely to fill up, but if you do run out of space, titles can be deleted from Kindle Library on your computer. What you need to be aware of is that only documents sent from your approved personal document list will ever be delivered to your Kindle devices. This is to prevent spam and marketing. The

good news is that your Kindle account on Amazon is used to manage not only the Kindle hardware itself, but also any Kindle reading devices like apps for iOS and Android or on the PC/Mac. Books purchased on one device or the website can then be delivered to any of the devices registered to the account. If you go out of Wi-Fi or 3G range, any items that have been requested or paid for but not yet downloaded can be found in the 'Pending Deliveries' section. To see all these options, you simply need to log in to your Kindle account on the Amazon website.

> "You have 5GB of storage space for personal documents"

Step-by-step | Delete a book or send it on

1: Access your account
Go to the Amazon website and log in with your email address and password. Click on 'Your Account', then 'Manage Your Kindle' in the panel on the right.

2: Select a book
This lists all the books in your Kindle Library. Newspapers, magazines and documents are shown on the left. Find the book you want and click on 'Actions'.

3: Delete or deliver
You can delete the eBook or send it on. Click 'Deliver to my…' for a drop-down list of your registered Kindle devices. Select the one you want and click 'Deliver'.

Power light

Why is the green power light blinking?

Ordinarily, the green power light on the Kindle only blinks when you are turning it on or off. If it starts blinking at other times, something's wrong. The main culprit is low battery power. Plug it in and charge it for an hour and it should be fine. If it's still blinking afterwards, it's a sign that there is a fault. No need to panic just yet: it could be that the first step, a restart, will fix the problem. If, after restarting the Kindle, the problem still remains then the next stage is to restore it to factory defaults. This clears everything out, including anything that can be causing a problem. It does mean you will have to re-register the Kindle and download all your purchased eBooks again, though. If that doesn't clear the problem then it's hardware related and you need to phone Amazon customer services to ask for a replacement.

■ *If you need to restart, you'll have to re-register your device*

Step-by-step | Fixing the flashing green light

1: The software solution
Press the Home button and then the Menu button. Navigate down to 'Settings' and select it. Then press the Menu button again. Navigate to 'Restart' and select it.

2: Go for a restart
If that didn't work then when it restarts, press Home and then Menu again. Go back into 'Settings' and press the Menu button again. This time select 'Restore to Factory Defaults'.

3: Restart and hope!
The Kindle will now be wiped clean, so after it reboots you will need to re-register yourself as the owner, set up the Wi-Fi and download your books from the Archive.

"If the green light is still blinking after charging, it's a sign that there is a fault"

Registration

My Kindle is registered to the wrong person. How can this be rectified?

This is a very common issue that comes up because Amazon automatically assumes that the person buying the Kindle is going to be the owner. When you buy it as a gift for someone, your Amazon account automatically gets a Kindle section added. It can also happen if you buy one second-hand from someone and they have forgotten to reset all the data on the Kindle so you are stuck with their name and details. In all these cases the solution is to deregister the Kindle, which removes the current owner's name and payment details as well as any content they have loaded to the device. This includes purchased eBooks and any documents transferred by USB. So, if you do buy one second-hand, you won't have to spend ages trying to clean it up; or equally, when selling, it's a simple process to get it ready to send to the new owner.

Step-by-step | Wipe clean the owner record

1: Deregister the device
Press the Home button then Menu. Navigate down to 'Settings' and select it. The first option is to 'Deregister' the device; select it to start the process.

2: Complete the clean
You'll be asked to confirm the action and warned that the Kindle won't do much until it gets re-registered. Confirm and it'll reset the ownership of the device.

3: Add the owner
The registration sequence will then come up. Enter your Amazon name and password, which will then link the Kindle to your account. You may need to add your Wi-Fi network.

Deleted book

What can I do if I accidentally delete an eBook?

The Amazon Whispersync system helps out here. You can never really get rid of anything accidentally because it's backed up on the Amazon server itself. If you remove an eBook from your Kindle, it immediately goes to the Archive – as long as there's an internet connection. Although files are listed in the Archive on your Kindle, they are actually stored on the Amazon server. It means all you need to do is select any item in the Archive and it will be downloaded back onto the Kindle again. Personal documents sent using the Amazon email address for your Kindle are also stored on the server and can be retrieved from the Archive. However, documents you transferred yourself via USB from a PC are not stored. That's why the option for eBooks reads 'Remove from device' and the same option for documents like this reads 'Delete this document'.

Step-by-step | Removing items and retrieving them

1: Removing an eBook
To remove an eBook from your Kindle, highlight it with the cursor and press the left move arrow. If you press the right one you get all the options for that file.

2: Into the Archive
Press 'Confirm' and the file will immediately go from the list and the Archive will suddenly say it has one more file. If you delete a USB-transferred document, it is simply deleted.

3: Back into play
Scroll down the list of books and select the 'Archive'. Move the cursor to the eBook you want back again. Press the right cursor arrow to add the book back to the Home list.

Slow webpages
Webpages are slow and hard to read – what can be done?

The web browser on the Kindle is experimental so it's a bit rough. It doesn't support Flash video, so don't go on sites expecting to be able to play them. It's not that much of a loss for Kindle 4 owners anyway because Amazon dispensed with the audio facilities that were in the Kindle 3 Keyboard. Some sites will look reasonable and how you would expect, while others can be all over the place. You get a large zoom cursor to move around the page until you get somewhere you want to look at. Then you zoom into that area and can navigate the cursor rather lumpily around the page. It's good enough to pick up data entry fields so it's usable. Some websites, though, can be hard to read and slow to load as well. Disabling JavaScript and images will speed it up considerably and you can tweak the settings to make it easier to view.

Step-by-step | Enhance your web browsing experience

1: Launch browser
Press the Home button and then Menu. Scroll down to 'Experimental' and select it. Select the web browser to launch it and use one of the bookmarks.

2: Make it bigger
Press Menu when on a webpage, select 'Change Font Size' and then in the options, change it to 150%. That will make the text much easier to read.

3: Disable these options
To make webpages load faster, press Menu and select 'Browser Settings'. Select 'Disable Javascript' and 'Disable Images'.

■ *There are ways to improve the usability of the experimental web browser*

Your Kindle glossary

We guide you through the features and terms that you're likely to encounter while using your Kindle

1-Click Payment

This is the quick payment method that you use to buy items from the Kindle Store and many other online storefronts. You can set this up from the Amazon website.

■ *The 1-Click Payment method makes purchasing items very easy indeed*

Five-way controller

This is the directional controller on any Kindle device that you use to navigate the various menus. It consists of four directional arrows and a central button that you press to make your selections.

Amazon

The online store and Kindle manufacturer. You will need to create a login to an Amazon account to purchase books and other digital literature on your Kindle device.

Back button

Present on all Kindle devices that, it takes you back to the previous screen to the one you are currently on.

Collections

These are collectives for how you organise your downloaded items. You can create and name new collections and then move particular items into them in order to help organise the home screen of your device and find things more easily.

E-Ink

The high-contrast display that is evident in all Kindle devices, on which pages read like real paper, and there is no screen glare, even in direct sunlight.

Experimental

This is a menu option on Kindle Keyboard

> Sex And Drugs And Rock 'n' Roll: The...
>
> **1**
> **UPMINSTER KID**
>
> *"My mum got the milk train down to Truro because they told her I wasn't going to make it. It was in Nissen huts, barrack huts, an RAF-type hospital, and they let her come to the outside, and they turned the light on over my bed – you know, she saw my little white face on the pillow: a four o'clock in the morning job. But I was still there the next morning."*
>
> *– Ian Dury*
>
> "Good Evening, I'm-from Essex, in case you couldn't tell," Ian growls, prompting roars of approval from the audience. "My given name is Dickie, I come from Billericay, and I'm doing very well." A few jaunty notes on the piano and Ian Dury and The Blockheads carry their fans off on a carousel ride of music hall and Essex laddism, courtesy of one of Ian's best loved lyrical creations, 'Billericay Dickie'. From his earliest dalliance with rock'n'Roll through to his very last gigs, Ian became universally identified with his characteristic stage persona. Off stage, in interviews and conversation, he cultivated a roguish image and his
>
> 32%

■ *The E-Ink display allows for a more impressive screen quality than ever before*

devices that allows users to sample features that are currently in development and provide feedback. These features include a web browser, Text-to-Speech capabilities and the ability to play MP3s as background music.

GSM

The Kindle Keyboard 3G uses GSM technology – the most popular mobile wireless standard – with wireless coverage in over 100 countries and territories, such as Australia, Hong Kong, Germany, Japan, Norway, Spain, South Africa, the United States and many others. On Kindle 3s you get free 3G, meaning you can connect to the Kindle Store anywhere in the world.

Home button

This is a button present on all Kindle devices that, when pressed, will instantly transport you to your Kindle Home screen.

Home screen

The default screen of your Kindle device where all of your purchased and downloaded content is selectable from.

Keyboard

Keyboards are what you use to type text and numbers on your Kindle device. The Kindle 3 comes with an integrated physical keyboard as standard, and the Kindle 4 has a Keyboard button that you can press to call up a virtual keyboard to type with.

Kindle Store

This is the online bookstore arm of Amazon where you can purchase and download books, newspapers, magazines and blogs for your Kindle device.

■ *The Kindle is relatively light on jargon, but there are still a few technical terms*

Menu button

This is a button present on all Kindle devices that, when pressed, will present a list of options that are native to the screen you are currently on.

Micro-USB/power port

Attach the USB cord that comes with your Kindle device into the micro-USB/power port and into the Kindle power adapter. Plug the adapter into a UK-compatible wall socket to charge the Kindle battery. You can also charge your Kindle by detaching the USB cord from the power adaptor and connecting it to a computer's USB port or powered USB hub.

Read-to-Me

With the Text-to-Speech feature, Kindle Keyboard can read English newspapers, magazines, blogs and books out loud. You can switch back and forth between reading and listening, with your spot being automatically saved. Pages automatically turn while the content is being read so you can listen hands-free. You can also choose from both male and female voices, which can be sped up or slowed down to suit your preference.

Registration

Kindles need to be registered to an Amazon account so that you can access the Kindle Store directly from the device and purchase books and items, which are then transferred directly to your Kindle.

Sample

When browsing for books on the Kindle Store you will be able to download free samples to your device, including a generous amount of pages that you can read on your device and get a feel for the book before buying it.

Wi-Fi

Wi-Fi (Wireless Fidelity) refers to a wireless networking system that uses any of the 802.11 wireless networking protocols. In order to use the features on your Kindle you must connect it to a wireless network.

Wish List

An online list to which you can add books and items from the Amazon store. This list is synced to your Amazon account and can be shared via email, Facebook or Twitter.

Whispernet

Whispernet utilises Amazon's optimised technology to enable you to wirelessly discover and download content. Your books, magazines and newspapers are delivered via Whispernet in less than 60 seconds.

Whispersync

Amazon's wireless syncing service. Your Kindle books can be read on Kindle, iPhone, iPad, PC, Mac, Android and Windows Phone 7 devices. Whispersync syncs your place across devices, so you can pick up where you left off.

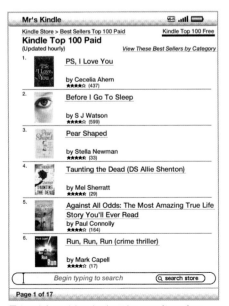

■ *Search for and download a wide range of items from the Kindle Store*

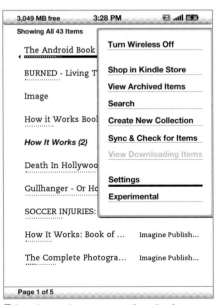

■ *From the menu button you can call up a list of options native to the device you are using*

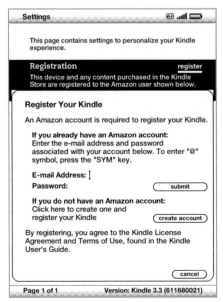

■ *It's important for you to register your device before you get started*

Index

Key pick
Page 47
Make sure everyone knows it's your Kindle by naming it so

Key pick
Page 92
Never miss a newspaper again by subscribing through Kindle

Key pick
Page 120
Get your Kindle connected
to Facebook and Twitter
and share eBooks

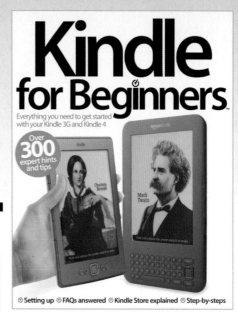

Not just for dummies

for Beginners

A clear, comprehensive series for people who want to start learning about iPhone, iPad, Mac, Android and Photoshop

Also in this series

Bookazines
eBooks · Apps
www.imaginebookshop.co.uk

High street

Kindle Store

ImagineShop.co.uk

App Store